HOUSE
30 Days
Savings
Challenges

Saving $210 in 30 Days
Start date : __/__/____   Finish date : __/__/____
Great work !!
Start
Each cloud = $7

Savings Challenges

Saving money is made easier and more enjoyable with this awesome savings challenges that will help you stay motivated on your saving journey.
Use this collection of Money Saving Challenge trackers to help you save for those unexpected expenses and make the savings a habit in life.

This incredible challenges bundle will help you Keep track of your progress as you crush your money-saving goals!

There are various interesting Challenges designed to make your saving journey fun and enjoyable. You can navigate the challenges through their time duration, total Saving amount, or per saving amount. Following are the awesome saving challenges included.

-- Summary --

30 Days Money Saving Challenges
- **$7** Savings Challenge (Save **$210**) .... 2 Challenges
- **$17** Savings Challenge (Save **$510**) .... 2 Challenges
- **$35** Savings Challenge (Save **$1050**) .... 2 Challenges
- Set Your Own Challenges .... 4 Challenges

60 Days Money Saving Challenges
- **$1** Savings Challenge (Save **$60**) .... 2 Challenges
- **$2** Savings Challenge (Save **$120**) .... 2 Challenges
- **$3** Savings Challenge (Save **$180**) .... 2 Challenges
- **$4** Savings Challenge (Save **$240**) .... 2 Challenges
- **$5** Savings Challenge (Save **$300**) .... 2 Challenges
- **$10** Savings Challenge (Save **$600**) .... 2 Challenges
- **$15** Savings Challenge (Save **$900**) .... 2 Challenges
- **$20** Savings Challenge (Save **$1200**) .... 2 Challenges
- **$30** Savings Challenge (Save **$1800**) .... 2 Challenges
- **$40** Savings Challenge (Save **$2400**) .... 2 Challenges
- **$50** Savings Challenge (Save **$3000**) .... 2 Challenges
- Set Your Own Challenges .... 4 Challenges

100 Days Money Saving Challenges
- **$10** Savings Challenge (Save **$500**) .... 2 Challenges
- **$20** Savings Challenge (Save **$1000**) .... 2 Challenges
- **$40** Savings Challenge (Save **$2000**) .... 2 Challenges
- **$80** Savings Challenge (Save **$4000**) .... 2 Challenges
- Set Your Own Challenges .... 4 Challenges

-- Summary --

26 Weeks (6 Months) Money Saving Challenges
- **+$1** Forward Savings Challenge (Save **$351**).... 2 Challenges
- **-$1** Backward Savings Challenge (Save **$351**).. 2 Challenges
- **+$3** Forward Savings Challenge (Save **$1053**).. 2 Challenges
- **-$3** Backward Savings Challenge (Save **$1053**) 2 Challenges
- **$2000** Savings Challenge .... 2 Challenges
- **$3000** Savings Challenge .... 2 Challenges
- **$4000** Savings Challenge .... 2 Challenges
- **$5000** Savings Challenge .... 2 Challenges
- **$10000** Savings Challenge .... 2 Challenges
- **$15000** Savings Challenge .... 2 Challenges
- Set Your Own Challenges .... 4 Challenges

52 Weeks (1 Year) Money Saving Challenges
- **$1000** Savings Challenge .... 2 Challenges
- **$2000** Savings Challenge .... 2 Challenges
- **$3000** Savings Challenge .... 2 Challenges
- **$4000** Savings Challenge .... 2 Challenges
- **$5000** Savings Challenge .... 2 Challenges
- **$10000** Savings Challenge .... 2 Challenges
- **$15000** Savings Challenge .... 2 Challenges
- **$20000** Savings Challenge .... 2 Challenges
- Set Your Own Challenges .... 4 Challenges

Each challenge has a starting point and a finishing point. However, only in some challenges, you need to follow a specific path, and in others you can choose your own path to reach the finishing point. Once you start a challenge, keep going, do not break, and always try to finish within the given time period. Per day/week saving amount is the same for some challenges and it is different for other challenges. So, depending on the challenge, choose the amount and save it for a particular week or day.

Once you have that amount saved, color the icon on each savings challenge and see your progress!

Happy Saving Journey!!

Saving $210 in 30 Days

Start date : __/__/____ Finish date : __/__/____

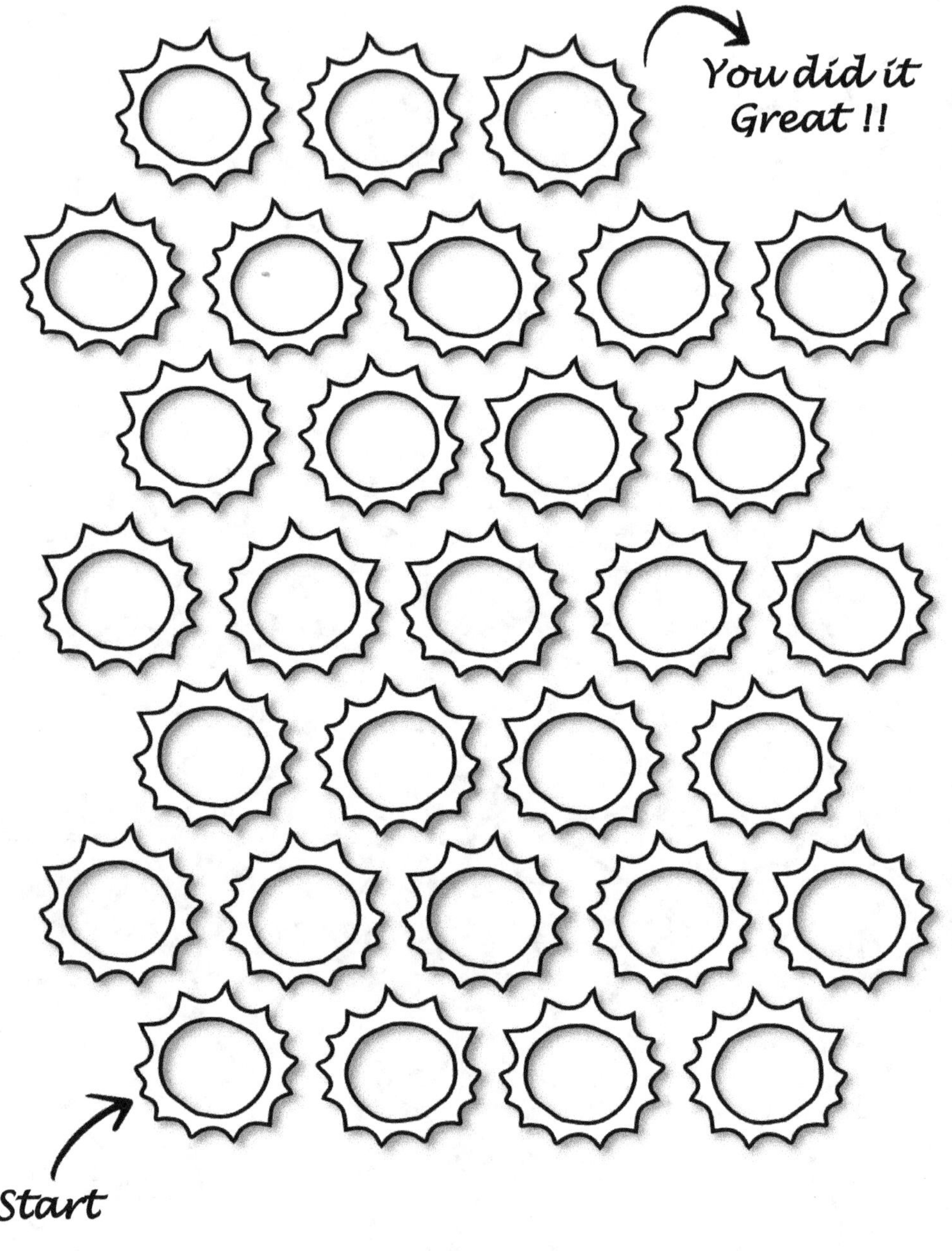

Saving $510 in 30 Days
Start date : __/__/____ Finish date : __/__/____
You did it
Great !!
Start
Each sun = $17

Saving $510 in 30 Days

Start date : __/__/____   Finish date : __/__/____

Each jar = $17

Saving $1050 in 30 Days
Start date : __/__/___   Finish date : __/__/___
Good Job!!
Start
Each leaf = $35

Saving $1050 in 30 Days

Start date : __/__/____   Finish date : __/__/____

Each leaf = $35

Set your own challenge
Saving $..... In 30 Days
Start date : __/__/____ Finish date : __/__/____
Great!!
Start
Each cloud = $....

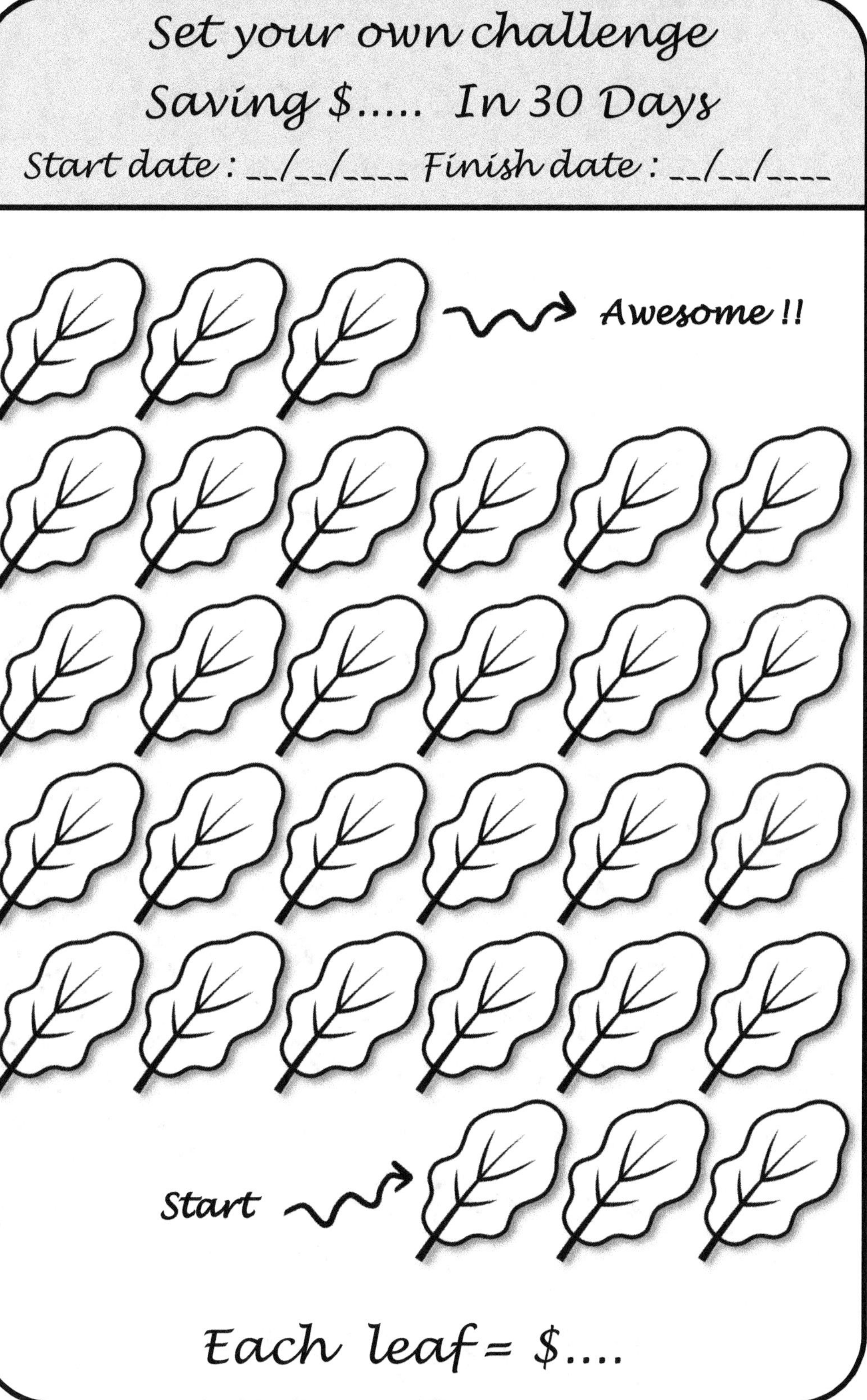

Set your own challenge
Saving $..... In 30 Days
Start date : __/__/____ Finish date : __/__/____
Awesome !!
Start
Each leaf = $....

Set your own challenge

Saving $.....   In 30 Days

Start date : __/__/___ Finish date : __/__/___

Set your own challenge

Saving $.....   In 30 Days

Start date : __/__/___   Finish date : __/__/___

Notes / Plans

60 Days
Savings
Challenges
HOUSE

Saving $60 in 60 Days ($1 per day)
Start date : __/__/____   Finish date : __/__/____
Start
Excellent!!
Each Coin = $1

Saving $60 in 60 Days ($1 per day)

Start date : __/__/____ Finish date : __/__/____

Start →

Good!

Saving $120 in 60 Days (\$2 per day)

Start date : __/__/____   Finish date : __/__/____

Saving $120 in 60 Days ($2 per day)

Start date : __/__/____   Finish date : __/__/____

Start

2$	2$	2$	2$	2$

2$	2$	2$	2$	2$	2$	2$
2$	2$	2$	2$	2$	2$	2$
2$	2$	2$	2$	2$	2$	2$
2$	2$	2$	2$	2$	2$	2$
2$	2$	2$	2$	2$	2$	2$
2$	2$	2$	2$	2$	2$	2$
2$	2$	2$	2$	2$	2$	2$
2$	2$	2$	2$	2$	2$	

Great!!

Saving $180 in 60 Days ($3 per day)

Start date : __/__/____   Finish date : __/__/____

Very
Good!!

Start

Saving $180 in 60 Days ($3 per day)

Start date : __/__/____   Finish date : __/__/____

Start

3$	3$	3$	3$	3$	3$
3$	3$	3$	3$	3$	3$
3$	3$	3$	3$	3$	3$
3$	3$	3$	3$	3$	3$
3$	3$	3$	3$	3$	3$
3$	3$	3$	3$	3$	3$
3$	3$	3$	3$	3$	3$
3$	3$	3$	3$	3$	3$
3$	3$	3$	3$	3$	3$
3$	3$	3$	3$	3$	3$

Fantastic!!

Saving $240 in 60 Days ($4 per day)
Start date : __/__/____   Finish date : __/__/____
Very Nice!
Start
Each rose = $4

Saving $240 in 60 Days (\$4 per day)

Start date : __/__/____   Finish date : __/__/____

4$	4$	4$	4$	4$	Great!!	
4$	4$	4$	4$	4$	4$	4$
4$	4$	4$	4$	4$	4$	4$
4$	4$	4$	4$	4$	4$	4$
4$	4$	4$	4$	4$	4$	4$
4$	4$	4$	4$	4$	4$	4$
4$	4$	4$	4$	4$	4$	4$
4$	4$	4$	4$	4$	4$	4$
Start	4$	4$	4$	4$	4$	4$

Saving $300 in 60 Days ($5 per day)

Start date : __ / __ / ____   Finish date : __ / __ / ____

5$ 5$ 5$ →   *Well Done!!*

5$ 5$ 5$ 5$ 5$ 5$

5$ 5$ 5$ 5$ 5$ 5$

5$ 5$ 5$ 5$ 5$ 5$

5$ 5$ 5$ 5$ 5$ 5$

5$ 5$ 5$ 5$ 5$ 5$

5$ 5$ 5$ 5$ 5$ 5$

5$ 5$ 5$ 5$ 5$ 5$

5$ 5$ 5$ 5$ 5$ 5$

5$ 5$ 5$ 5$ 5$ 5$

Start ⤳   5$ 5$ 5$

Saving $300 in 60 Days ($5 per day)
Start date : __/__/____   Finish date : __/__/____
Start
Good!
Each acorn = $5

Saving $600 in 60 Days ($10 per day)

Start date : __/__/____ Finish date : __/__/____

Saving $600 in 60 Days ($10 per day)

Start date : __/__/____   Finish date : __/__/____

Awesome!

10$ 10$ 10$ 10$ 10$

10$ 10$ 10$ 10$ 10$ 10$ 10$

10$ 10$ 10$ 10$ 10$ 10$ 10$

10$ 10$ 10$ 10$ 10$ 10$ 10$

10$ 10$ 10$ 10$ 10$ 10$ 10$

10$ 10$ 10$ 10$ 10$ 10$ 10$

10$ 10$ 10$ 10$ 10$ 10$ 10$

10$ 10$ 10$ 10$ 10$ 10$ 10$

Start

10$ 10$ 10$ 10$ 10$ 10$

Saving $900 in 60 Days ($15 per day)

Start date : __/__/____   Finish date : __/__/____

Start →

15$ 15$ 15$ 15$ 15$

15$ 15$ 15$ 15$ 15$ 15$ 15$

15$ 15$ 15$ 15$ 15$ 15$ 15$

15$ 15$ 15$ 15$ 15$ 15$ 15$

15$ 15$ 15$ 15$ 15$ 15$ 15$

15$ 15$ 15$ 15$ 15$ 15$ 15$

15$ 15$ 15$ 15$ 15$ 15$ 15$

15$ 15$ 15$ 15$ 15$ 15$ 15$

15$ 15$ 15$ 15$ 15$ 15$ Great!

Saving $900 in 60 Days *($15 per day)*

Start date : __/__/____   Finish date : __/__/____

Start ↙

15$	15$	15$	15$	15$	15$
15$	15$	15$	15$	15$	15$
15$	15$	15$	15$	15$	15$
15$	15$	15$	15$	15$	15$
15$	15$	15$	15$	15$	15$
15$	15$	15$	15$	15$	15$
15$	15$	15$	15$	15$	15$
15$	15$	15$	15$	15$	15$
15$	15$	15$	15$	15$	15$
15$	15$	15$	15$	15$	15$

Impressive!! ↙

Saving $1200 in 60 Days ($20 per day)
Start date : __/__/____   Finish date : __/__/____
Start
Each rose = $20
Good Job!!

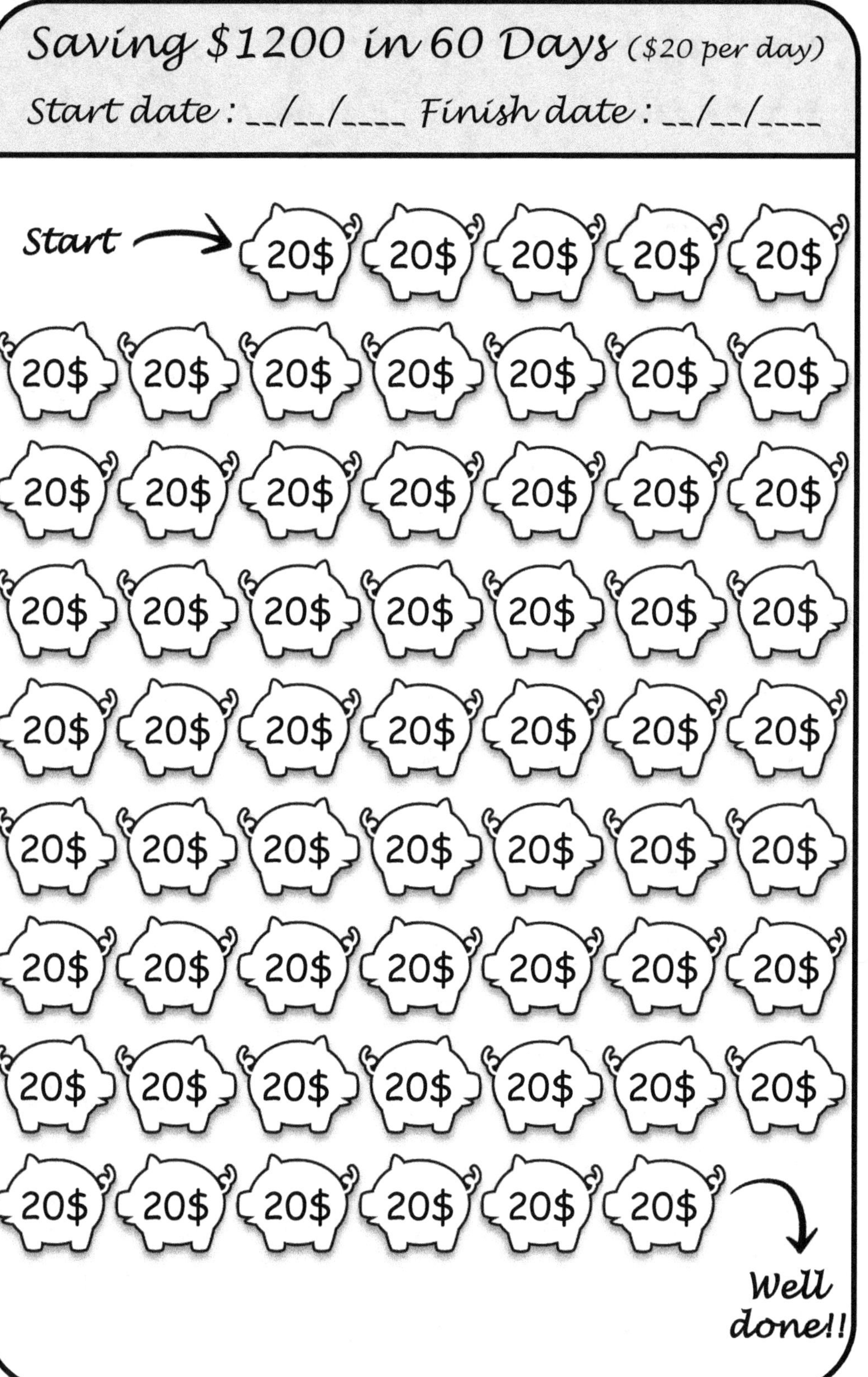

Saving $1200 in 60 Days ($20 per day)
Start date : __/__/____ Finish date : __/__/____
Start
20$ 20$ 20$ 20$ 20$
20$ 20$ 20$ 20$ 20$ 20$ 20$
20$ 20$ 20$ 20$ 20$ 20$ 20$
20$ 20$ 20$ 20$ 20$ 20$ 20$
20$ 20$ 20$ 20$ 20$ 20$ 20$
20$ 20$ 20$ 20$ 20$ 20$ 20$
20$ 20$ 20$ 20$ 20$ 20$ 20$
20$ 20$ 20$ 20$ 20$ 20$ 20$
20$ 20$ 20$ 20$ 20$ 20$
Well done!!

Saving $1800 in 60 Days ($30 per day)
Start date : __/__/____ Finish date : __/__/____
Start
Awesome!
Each leaf = $30

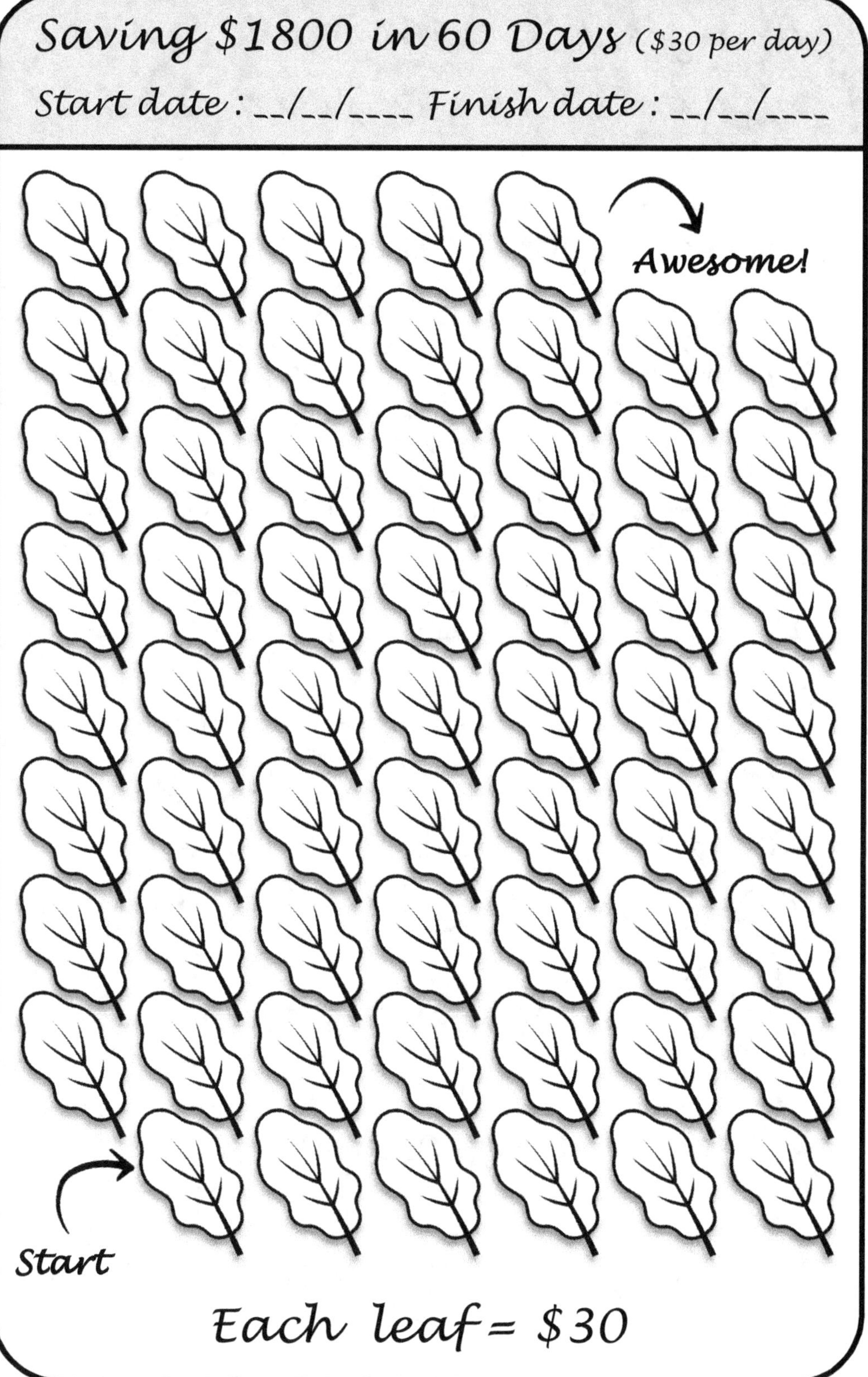

Saving $1800 in 60 Days ($30 per day)
Start date : __/__/____ Finish date : __/__/____
Awesome!
Start
Each leaf = $30

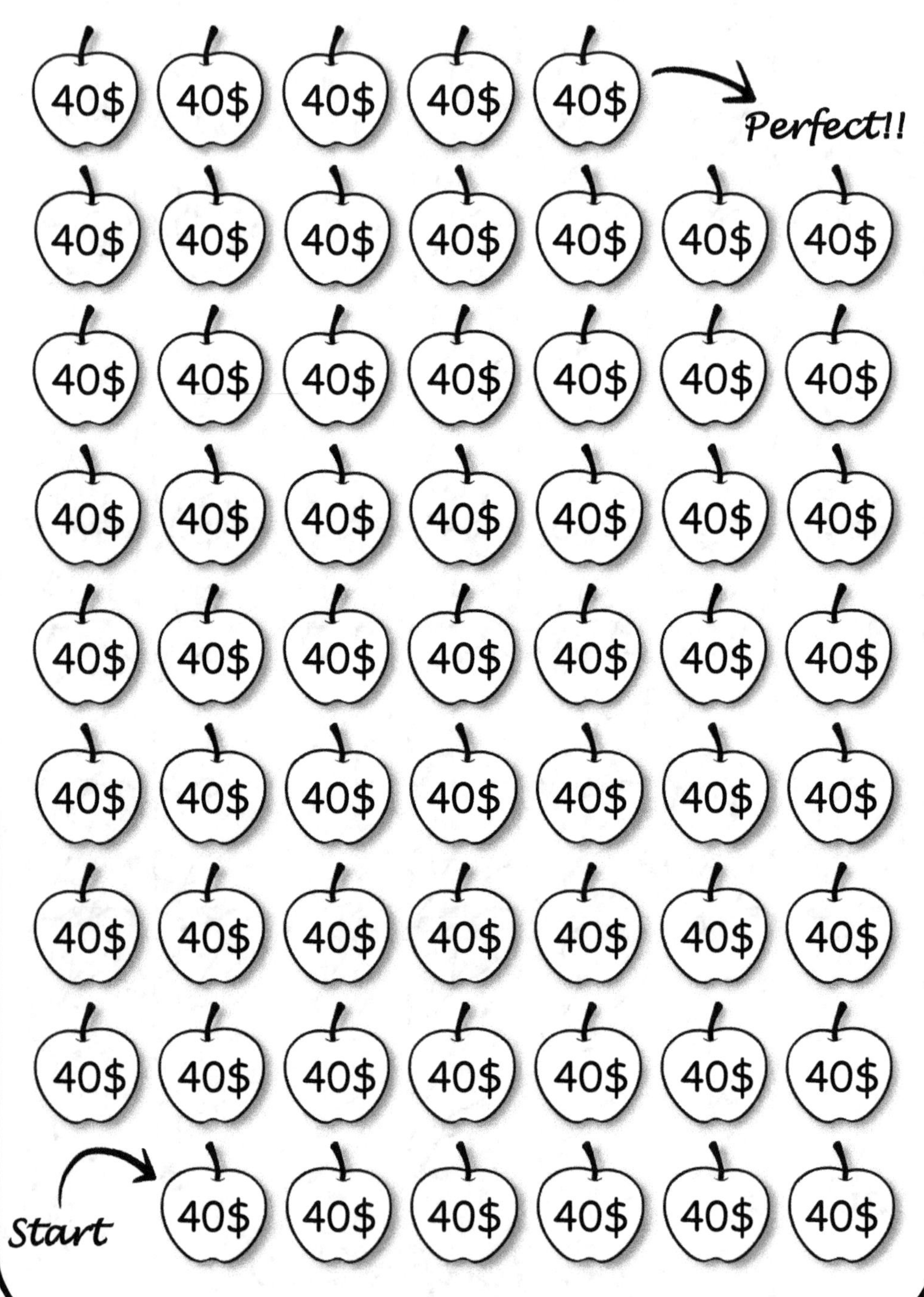

Saving $2400 in 60 Days ($40 per day)
Start date : __/__/____ Finish date : __/__/____
Perfect!!
40$
Start

Saving $2400 in 60 Days (\$40 per day)

Start date : __/__/____ Finish date : __/__/____

Start →

		40\$	40\$	40\$	40\$	40\$
40\$	40\$	40\$	40\$	40\$	40\$	40\$
40\$	40\$	40\$	40\$	40\$	40\$	40\$
40\$	40\$	40\$	40\$	40\$	40\$	40\$
40\$	40\$	40\$	40\$	40\$	40\$	40\$
40\$	40\$	40\$	40\$	40\$	40\$	40\$
40\$	40\$	40\$	40\$	40\$	40\$	40\$
40\$	40\$	40\$	40\$	40\$	40\$	40\$
40\$	40\$	40\$	40\$	40\$	40\$	

Awesome!

Saving $3000 in 60 Days ($50 per day)

Start date : __/__/____   Finish date : __/__/____

Each strawberry = $50

Saving $3000 in 60 Days ($50 per day)

Start date : __/__/____   Finish date : __/__/____

Start

Incredible!!

Each banana = $50

Set your own challenge

Saving $..... In 60 Days

Start date : __/__/____ Finish date : __/__/____

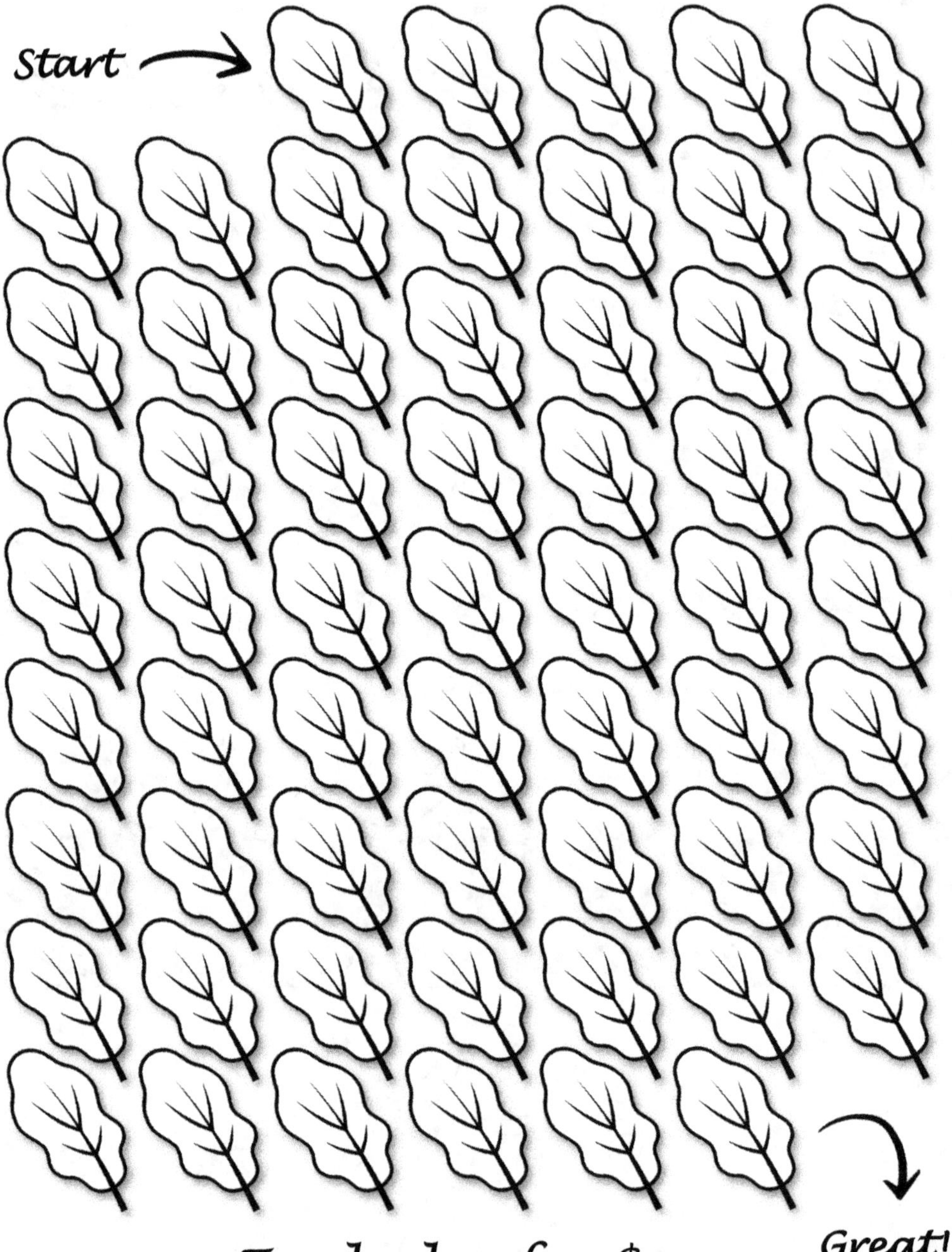

Start →

Each leaf = $....

Great!

Set your own challenge
Saving $..... In 60 Days

Start date : __/__/___ Finish date : __/__/___

Set your own challenge
Saving $..... In 60 Days
Start date : __/__/____ Finish date : __/__/____
Great job!!
Start
Each orange = $....

Set your own challenge
Saving $.....   In 60 Days
Start date : __/__/____ Finish date : __/__/____
Start
Good
work!!
Each lemon = $....

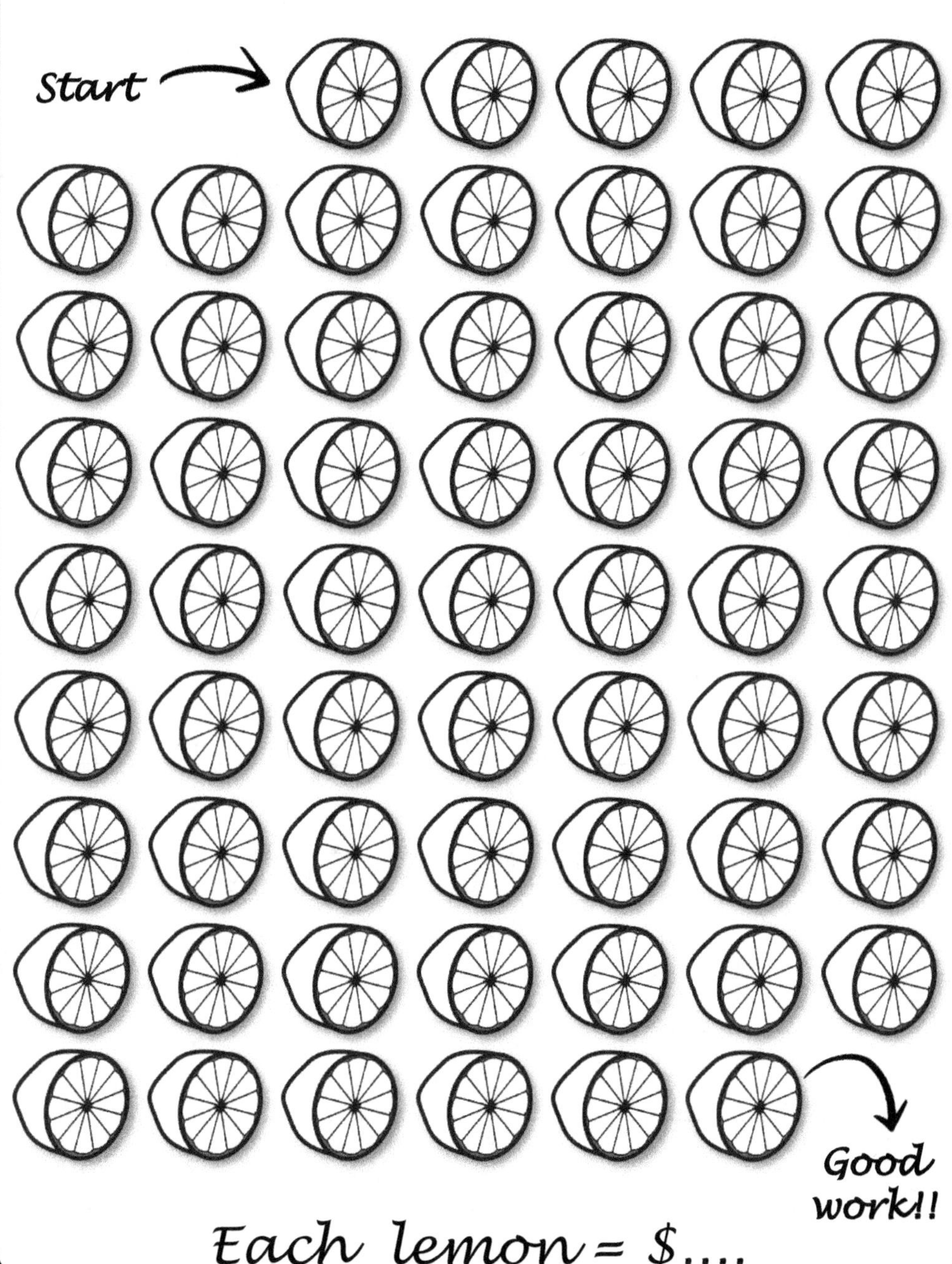

Notes / Plans

100 Days
Savings
Challenges
HOUSE

Saving $500 in 100 Days
Start date : __/__/____ Finish date : __/__/____
Well done!!
Start
Each hexagon (2 days) = $10

Saving $500 in 100 Days

Start date : __/__/____   Finish date : __/__/____

Start →

Congrats!!

Each heart (2 days) = $10

Saving $1000 in 100 Days

Start date : __/__/____ Finish date : __/__/____

Each rhombus (2 days) = $20

Saving $1000 in 100 Days

Start date : __/__/____ Finish date : __/__/____

Start →

Excellent!!

Each coin (2 days) = $20

Saving $2000 in 100 Days

Start date : __/__/____ Finish date : __/__/____

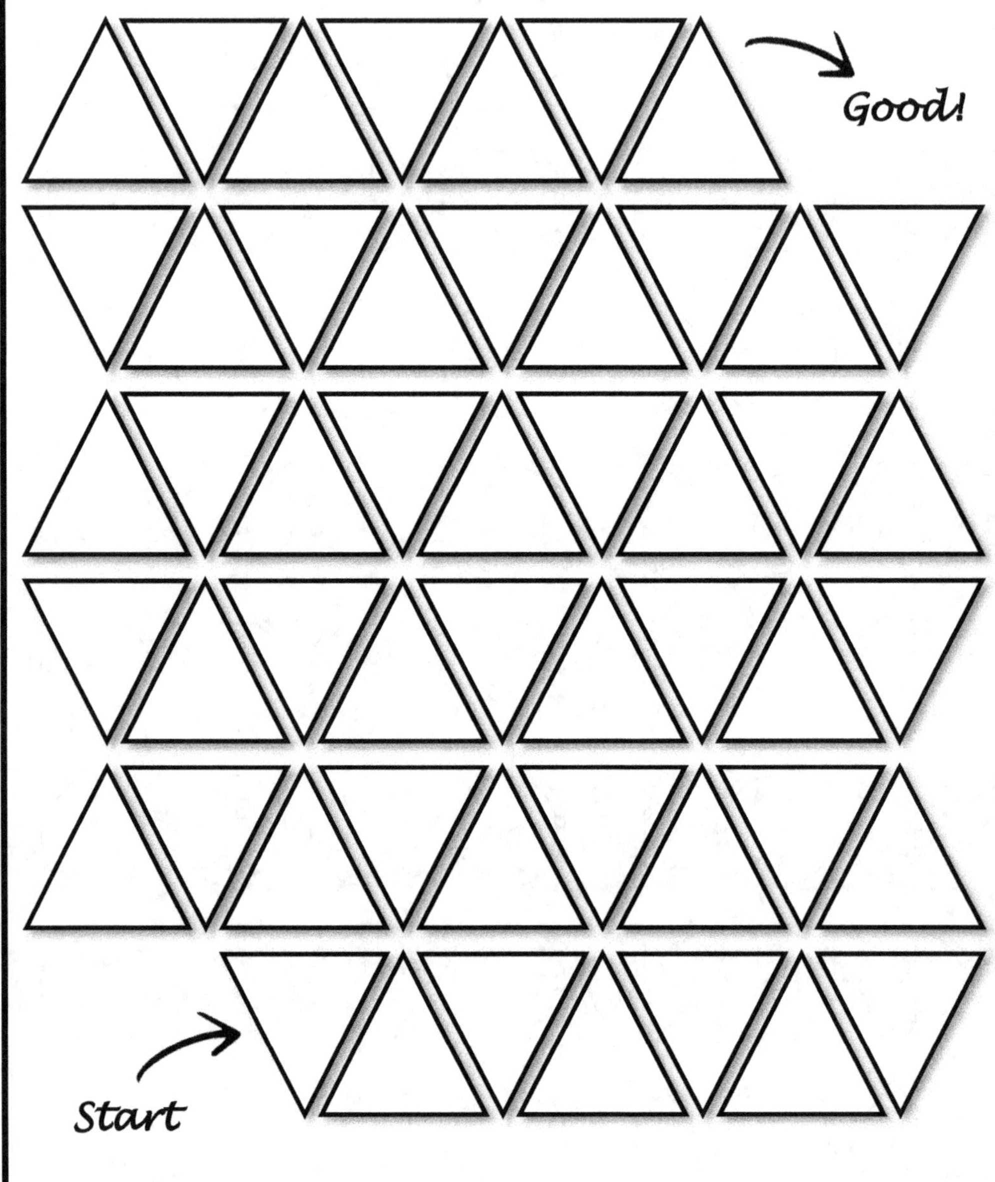

Each triangle (2 days) = $40

Saving $2000 in 100 Days

Start date : __/__/____ Finish date : __/__/____

Perfect!!

Start

Each pentagon *(2 days)* = $40

Saving $4000 in 100 Days

Start date : __/__/____ Finish date : __/__/____

Each rose (1 day) = $40

Saving $4000 in 100 Days

Start date : __/__/____ Finish date : __/__/____

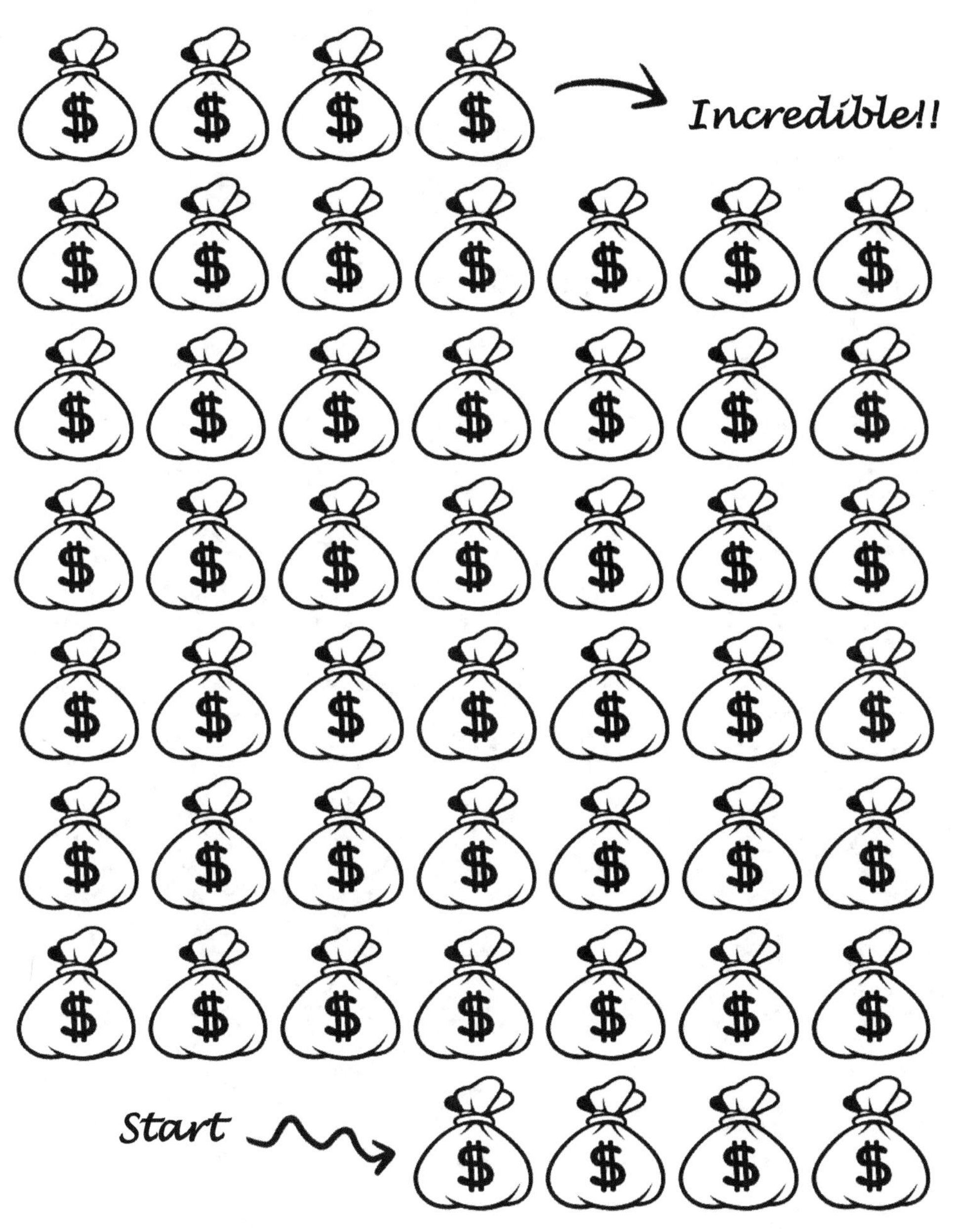

Each bag (2 days) = $80

Set your own challenge
Saving $..... In 100 Days
Start date : __/__/____ Finish date : __/__/____

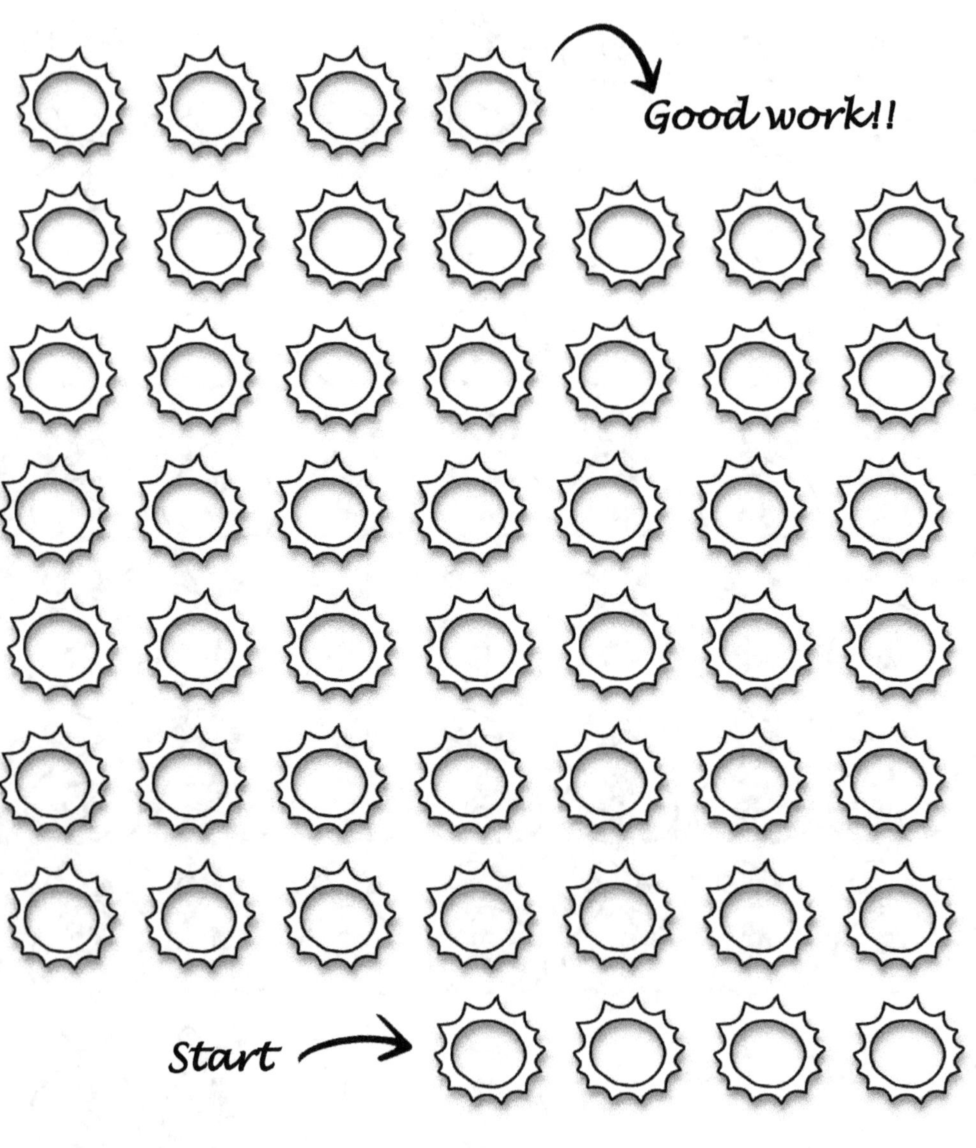

Good work!!
Start

Each sun (2 days) = $....

Set your own challenge
Saving $..... In 100 Days

Start date : __/__/___   Finish date : __/__/___

Each rose (2 days) = $....

Set your own challenge
Saving $..... In 100 Days

Start date : __/__/____ Finish date : __/__/____

Start here ⟿

Wow!!

Each leaf *(2 days)* = $....

Set your own challenge
Saving $..... In 100 Days

Start date : __/__/____ Finish date : __/__/____

Start ⟿

Nice Work!!

Each pig (1 day) = $....

Notes / Plans

26 Weeks
Savings
Challenges
HOUSE

Saving $351 in 26 Weeks

Start date : __/__/____   Finish date : __/__/____

+$1 Forward

Follow the increasing order from $1 to $26

Well done!!

Start

$26 $25 $24 $23 $22 $21 $20 $19 $18 $17 $16 $15 $14

$1 $2 $3 $4 $5 $6 $7 $8 $9 $10 $11 $12 $13

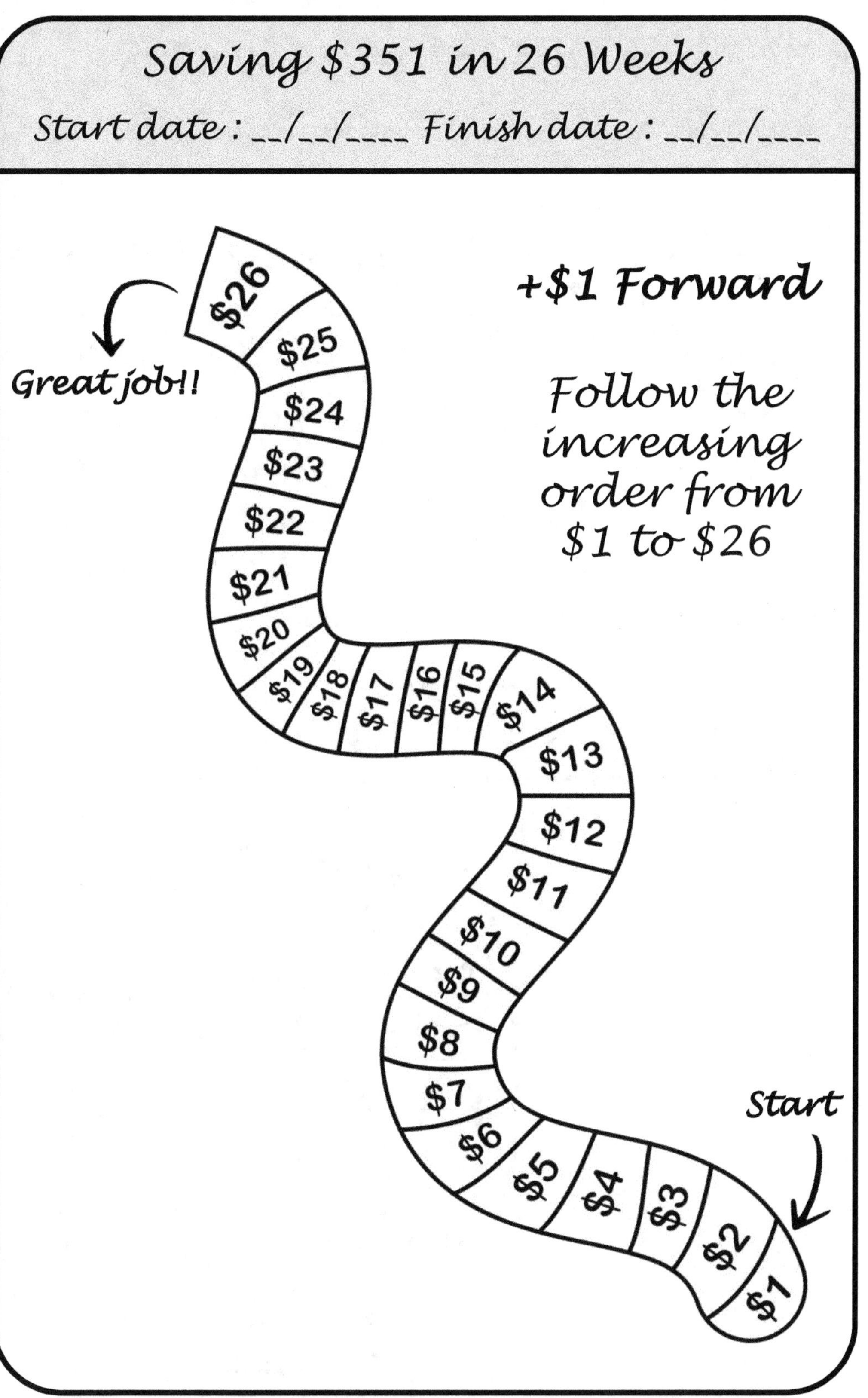

Saving $351 in 26 Weeks
Start date : __/__/____   Finish date : __/__/____
$26
$25
$24
$23
$22
$21
$20
$19
$18
$17
$16
$15
$14
$13
$12
$11
$10
$9
$8
$7
$6
$5
$4
$3
$2
$1
Great job!!
+$1 Forward
Follow the increasing order from $1 to $26
Start

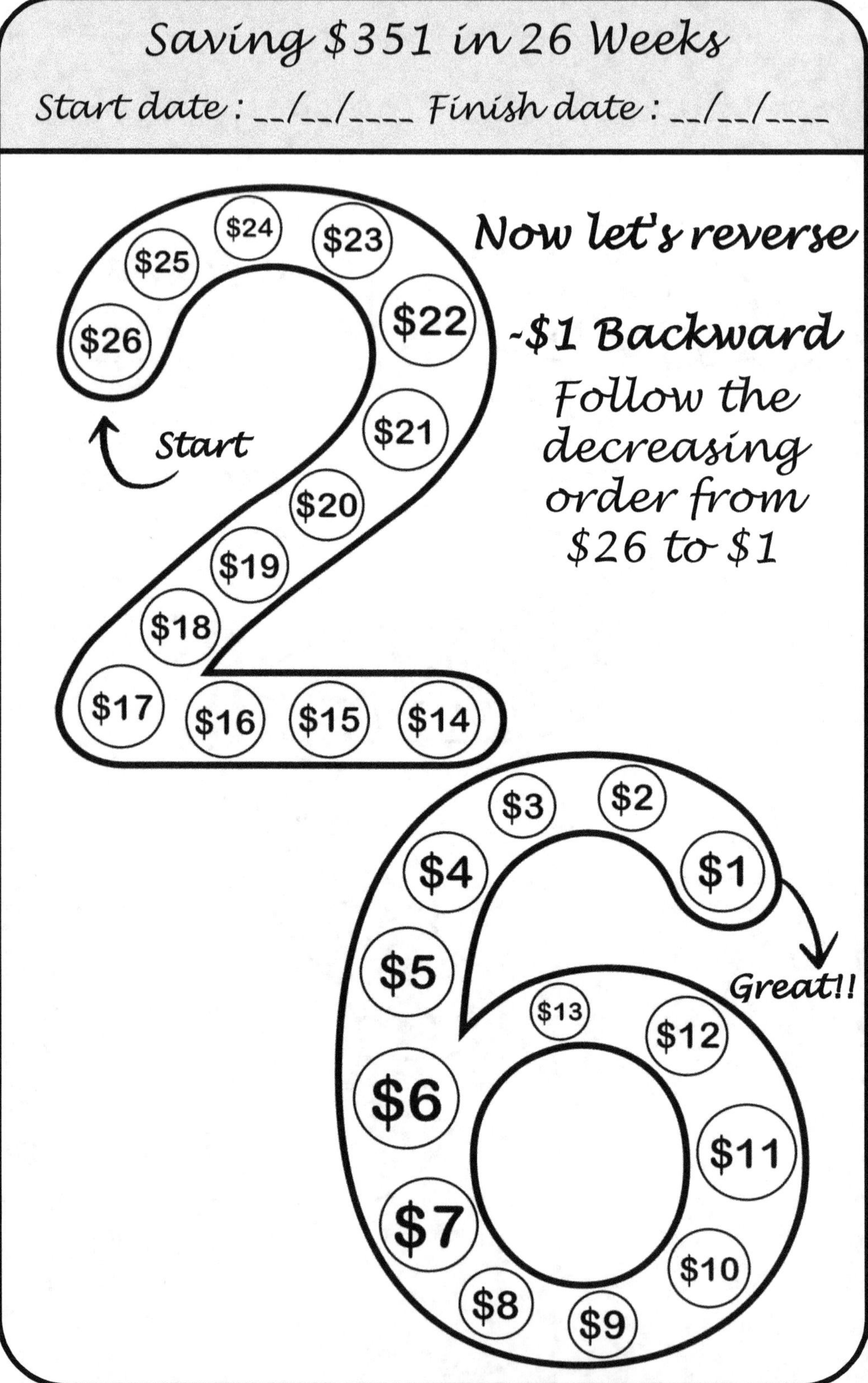

Saving $351 in 26 Weeks
Start date : __/__/____   Finish date : __/__/____
$25 $24 $23
$26 $22
Start $21
$20
$19
$18
$17 $16 $15 $14
Now let's reverse
-$1 Backward
Follow the decreasing order from $26 to $1
$3 $2
$4 $1
$5
$13 $12
$6
$11
$7
$10
$8 $9
Great!!

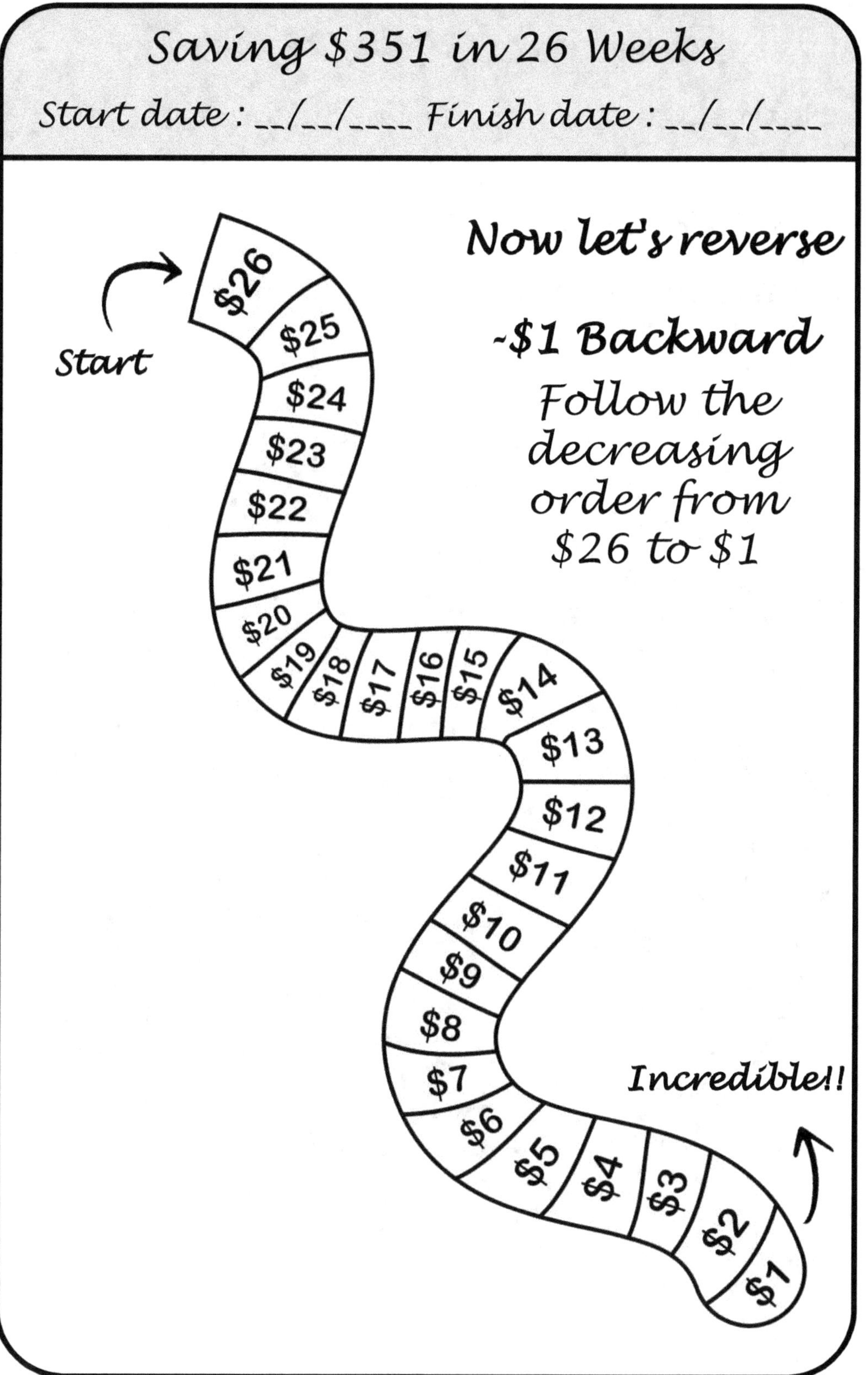

Saving $351 in 26 Weeks
Start date : __/__/____   Finish date : __/__/____
Start
$26
$25
$24
$23
$22
$21
$20
$19
$18
$17
$16
$15
$14
$13
$12
$11
$10
$9
$8
$7
$6
$5
$4
$3
$2
$1
Now let's reverse
-$1 Backward
Follow the decreasing order from $26 to $1
Incredible!!

+$3 Forward

Follow the increasing order from $3 to $78

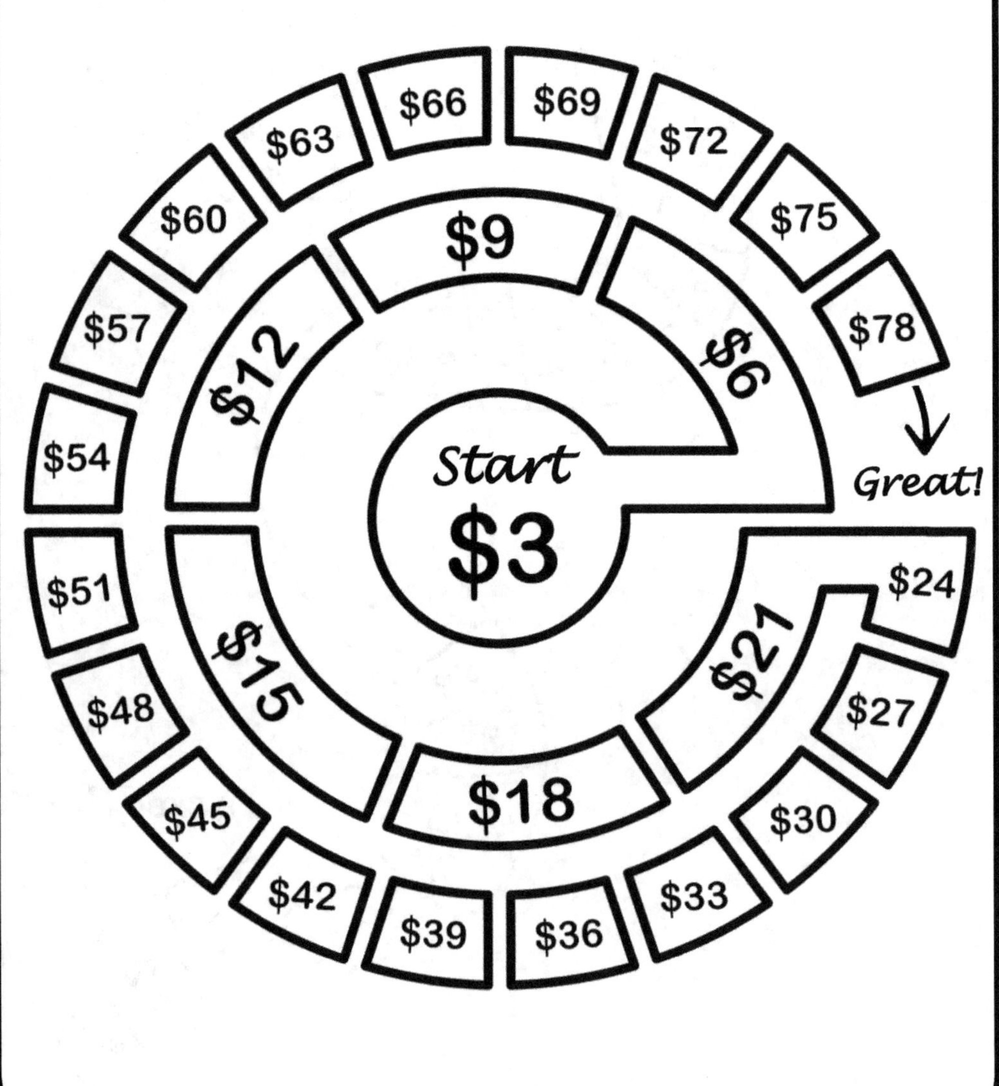

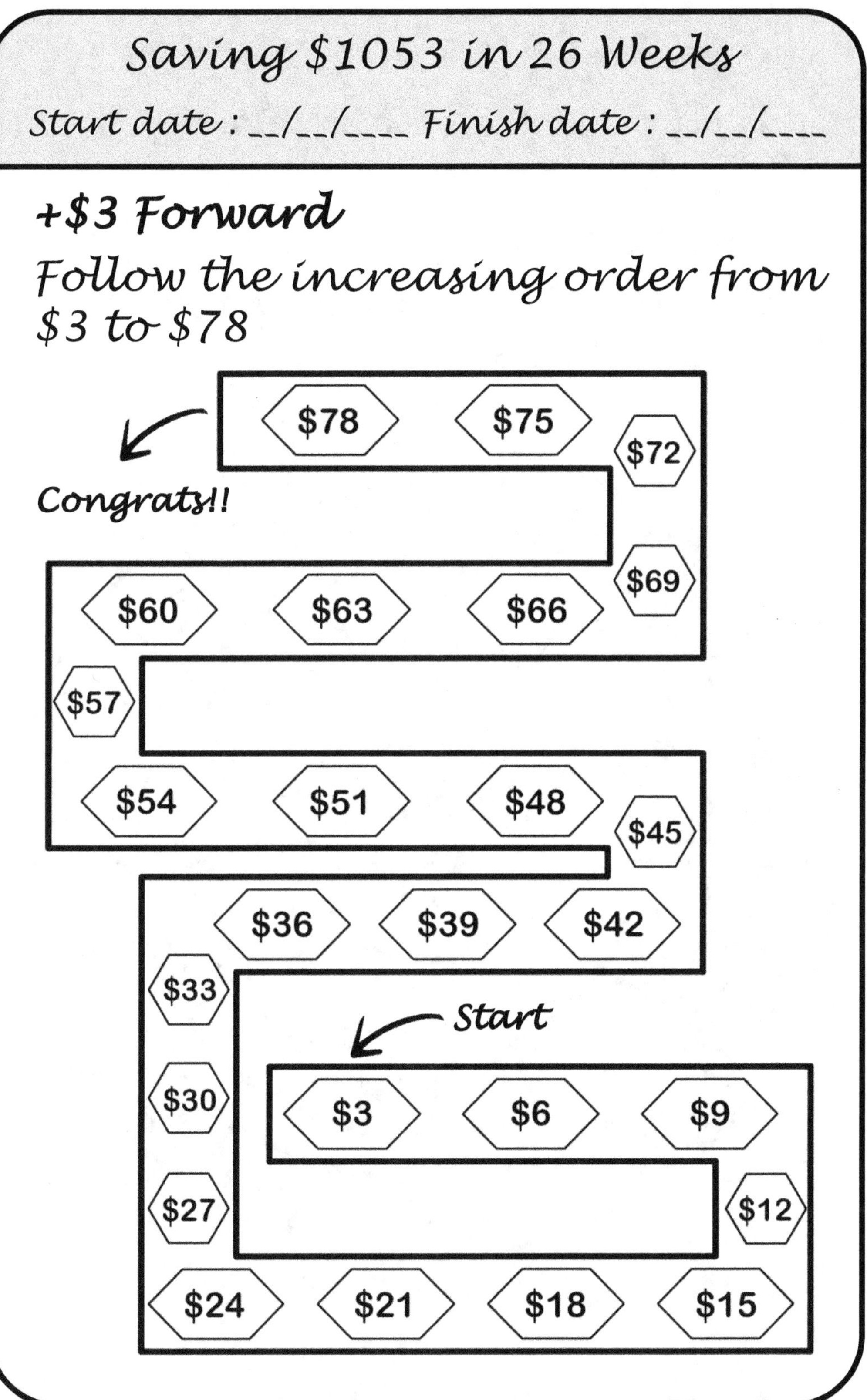

Saving $1053 in 26 Weeks
Start date : __/__/____   Finish date : __/__/____
+$3 Forward
Follow the increasing order from $3 to $78
$78
$75
$72
Congrats!!
$69
$60
$63
$66
$57
$54
$51
$48
$45
$36
$39
$42
$33
Start
$30
$3
$6
$9
$27
$12
$24
$21
$18
$15

Saving $1053 in 26 Weeks

~$3 Backward

Follow the decreasing order from $78 to $3

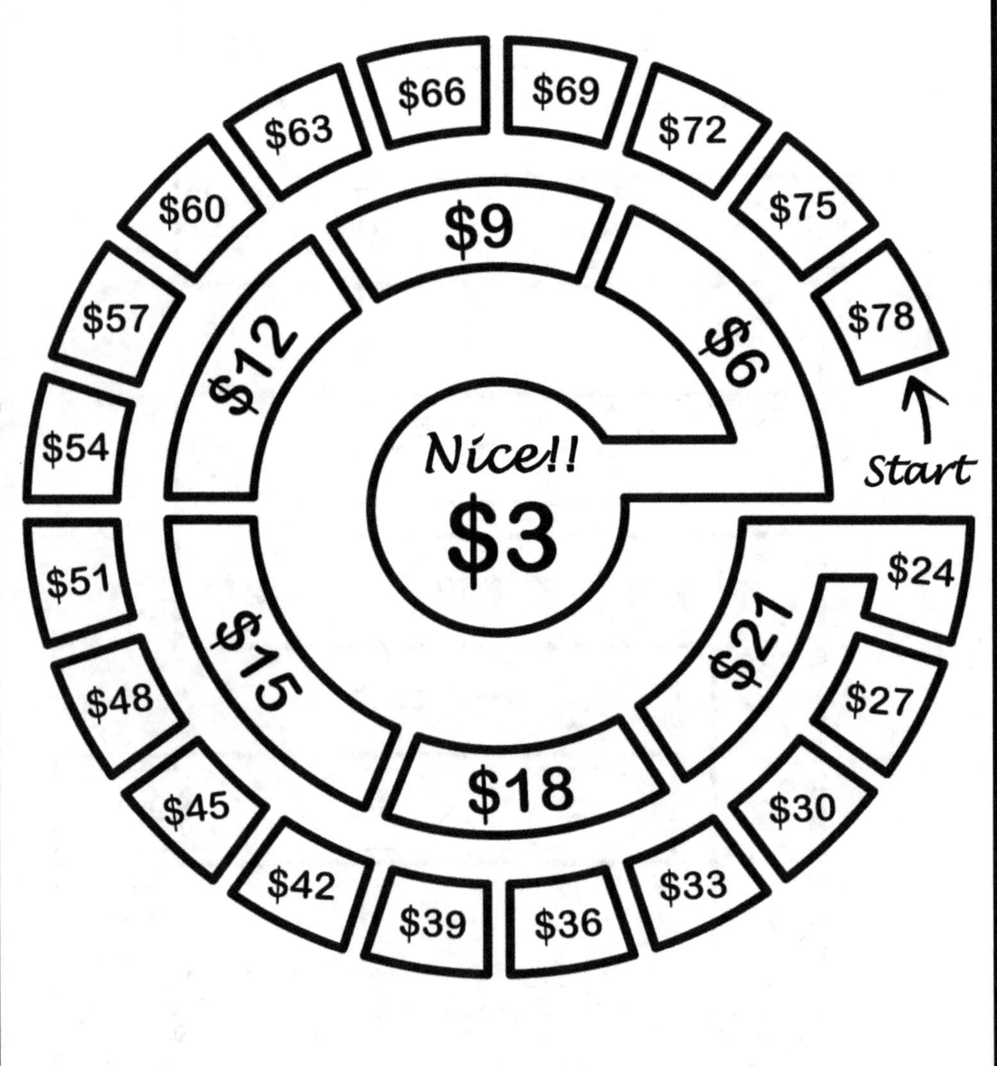

Saving $1053 in 26 Weeks

Start date : __/__/____ Finish date : __/__/____

-$3 Backward

Follow the decreasing order from $78 to $3

Saving $2000 in 26 Weeks

Start date : __/__/____   Finish date : __/__/____

1 Coin = 1 Week

Saving $2000 in 26 Weeks

Start date : __/__/____   Finish date : __/__/____

1 Leaf = 1 Week

Saving $3000 in 26 Weeks

Start date : __/__/____   Finish date : __/__/____

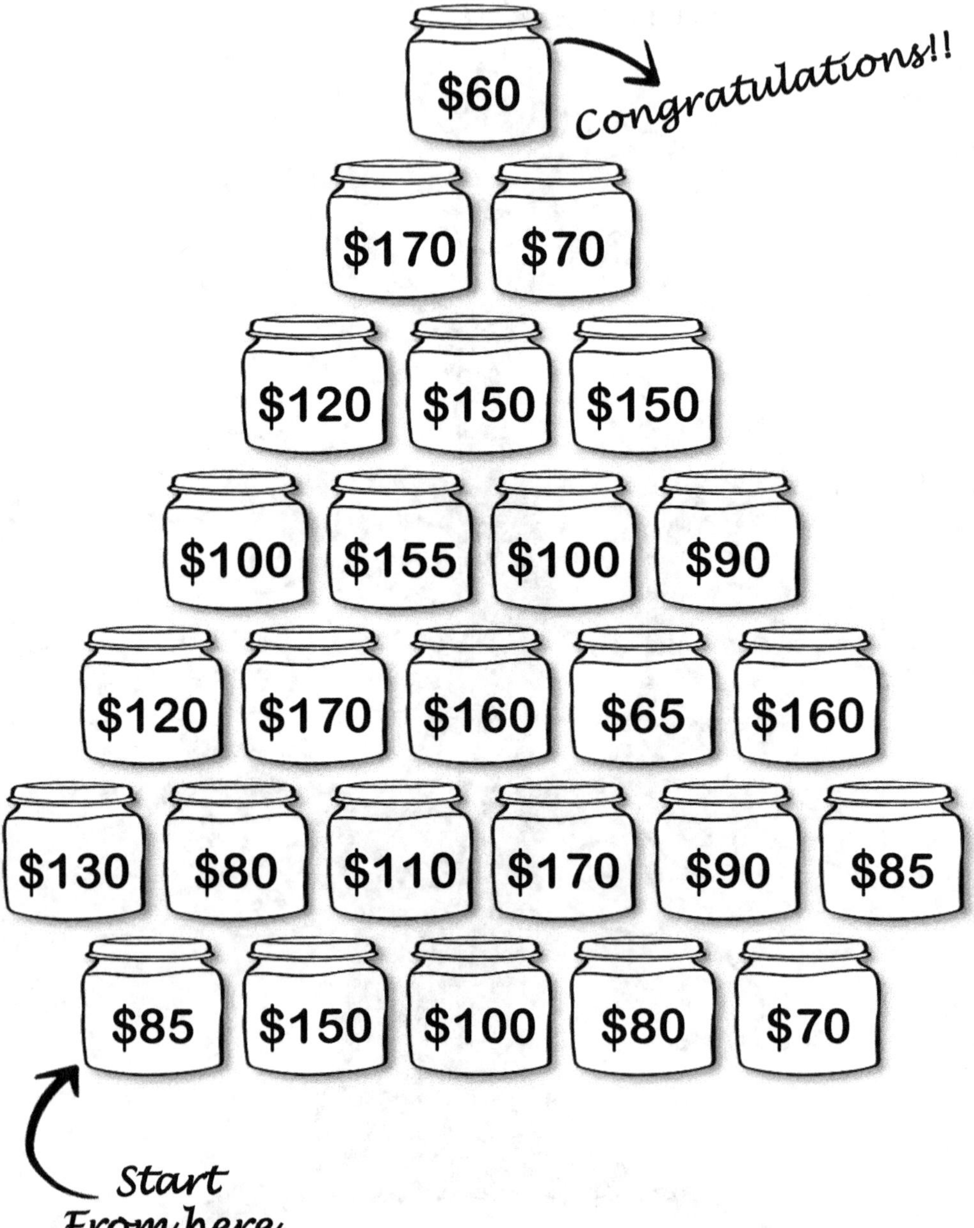

1 Jar = 1 Week

Saving $3000 in 26 Weeks

Start date : __/__/____ Finish date : __/__/____

Well done!!

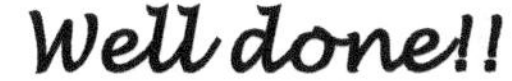

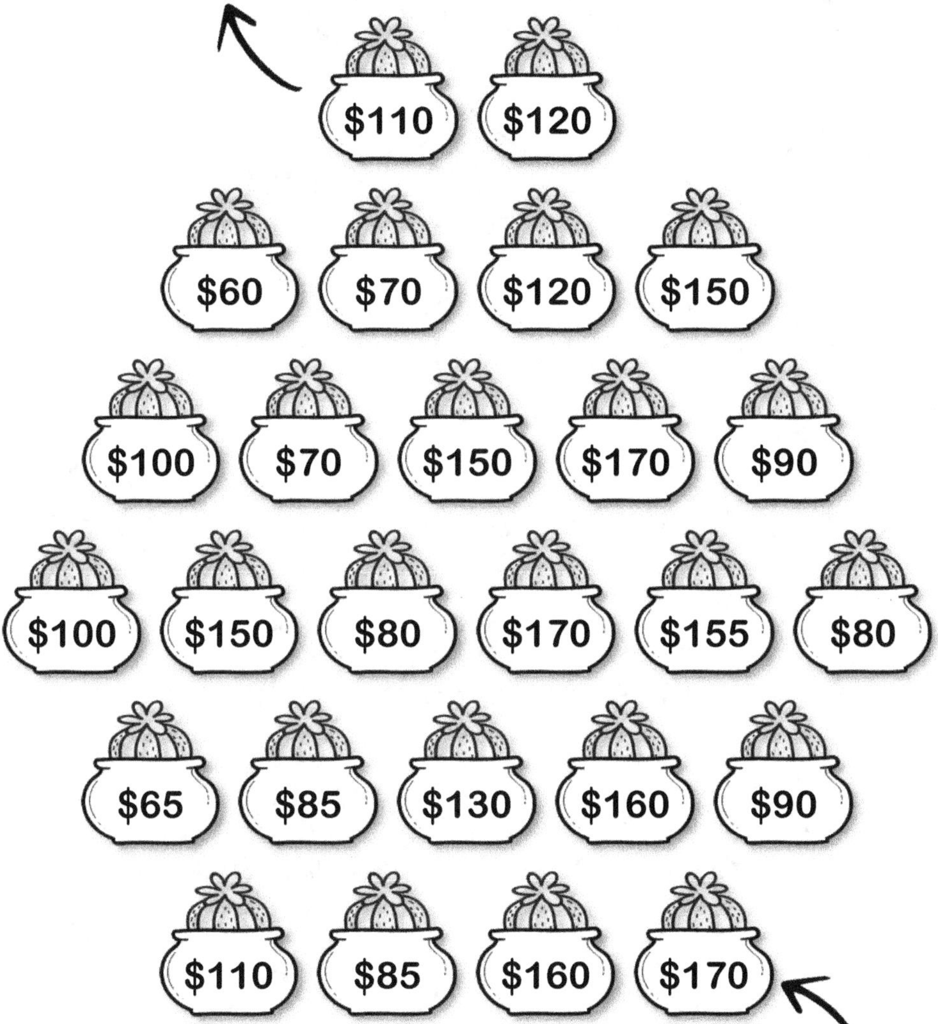
$110 $120
$60 $70 $120 $150
$100 $70 $150 $170 $90
$100 $150 $80 $170 $155 $80
$65 $85 $130 $160 $90
$110 $85 $160 $170

Let's Start Here

1 Plant = 1 Week

Saving $4000 in 26 Weeks

Start date : __/__/____ Finish date : __/__/____

1 Rhombus = 1 Week

Saving $4000 in 26 Weeks

Start date : __/__/____   Finish date : __/__/____

$140 $130 $170   *You did it, Great!!*

$110 $180 $170 $165

$160 $185 $150 $140

$180 $160 $155 $150

$180 $185 $170 $160

$140 $110 $100 $170

Let's Start Here → $150 $120 $170

1 Cloud = 1 Week

Saving $5000 in 26 Weeks
Start date : __/__/____   Finish date : __/__/____
Super work!!
$240
$220
$260
$200
$170
$195
$185
$150
$250
$180
$270
$230
$170
$160
$150
$180
$240
$150
$170
$160
$170
$165
$160
$155
$240
$180
Start
1 Plant = 1 Week

Saving $5000 in 26 Weeks
Start date : __/__/____   Finish date : __/__/____

Eat that money pill!!
Wow perfect!!
$150
$240
$200
$195
$220
$260
$170
$185
$150
$250
$180
$270
$160
$170
$230
$170
$160
$180
$160
$150
$240
$165
$240
$180
$170
$155
Start here
1 Pill = 1 Week

Saving $10.000 in 26 Weeks

Start date : __/__/____   Finish date : __/__/____

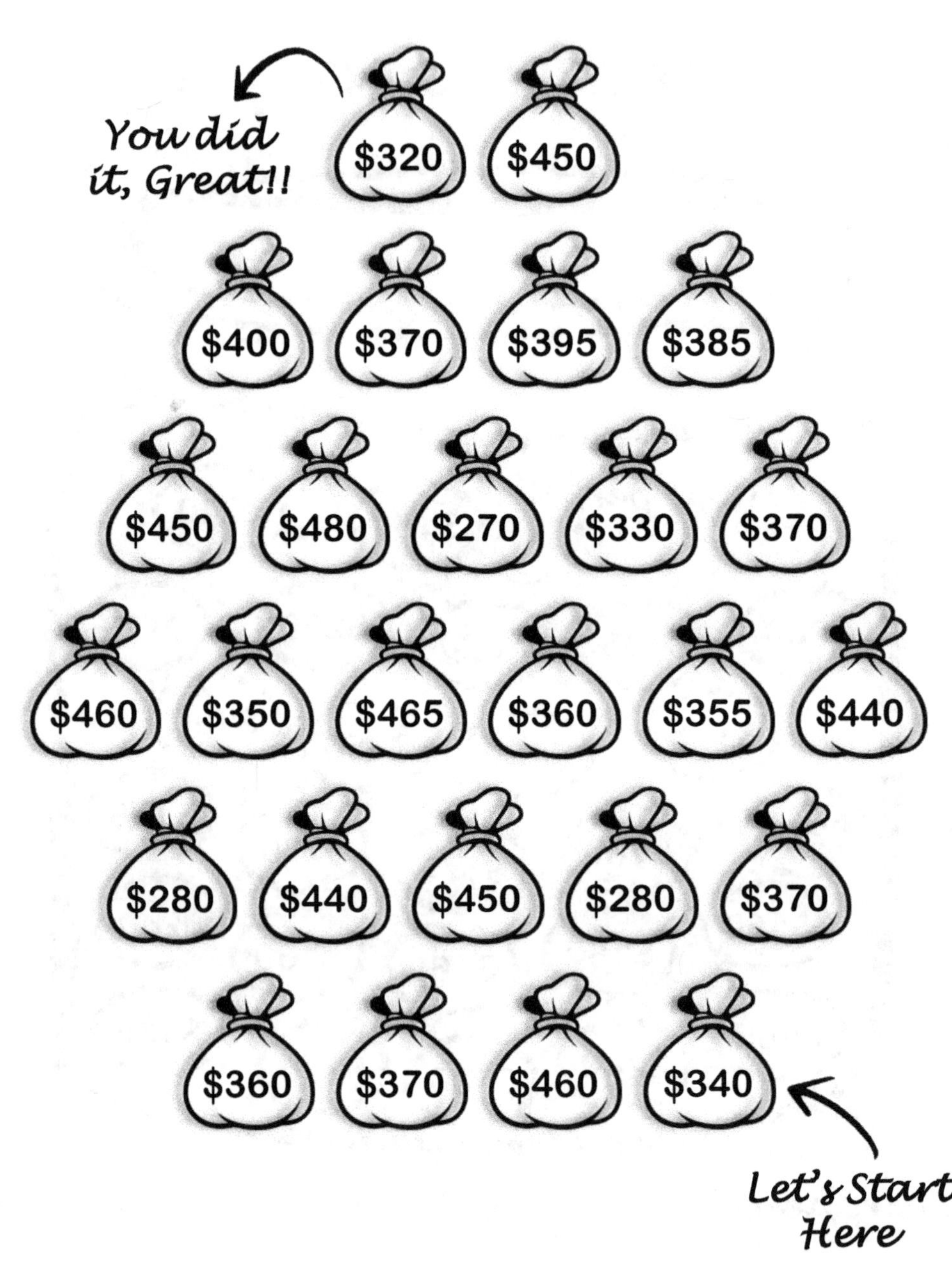

1 Bag = 1 Week

Saving $10.000 in 26 Weeks

Start date : __/__/____   Finish date : __/__/____

Great job!!

$320	$440	$450	$360	$370	$450

$340 $395 $370 $460

$350 $385

$450 $480

$460 $400

Start Here

$370 $270 $330 $465

$360 $355 $440 $280 $280 $370

1 Shape = 1 Week

Saving $15.000 in 26 Weeks
Start date : __/__/____   Finish date : __/__/____
$570
$620
Excellent job!!
$460
$500
$570
$595
$585
$650
$550
$580
$570
$630
$570
$460
$550
$565
$560
$555
$640
$580
$640
$650
$580
$570
$560
$640
Let's Start Here
1 Plant = 1 Week

Saving $15.000 in 26 Weeks
Start date : __/__/____   Finish date : __/__/____
$640
$570
$595
$585
Wow!!
$580
$570
$630
$570
$460
$550
$565
$560
$555
$640
$560
$570
$640
$580
$650
$570
$620
$460
$650
$550
Start Here
$580
$500
1 Plant = 1 Week

Set your own challenge
Saving $..... In 26 Weeks
Start date : __/__/____ Finish date : __/__/____
Well done!!
Start
1 Acorn = $....

Set your own challenge
Saving $..... In 26 Weeks

Start date : __/__/____ Finish date : __/__/____

Set your own challenge
Saving $..... In 26 Weeks
Start date : __/__/____ Finish date : __/__/____
Perfect!!
Let's Start Here
1 Plant = $....

Set your own challenge
Saving $..... In 26 Weeks
Start date : __/__/____ Finish date : __/__/____
Incredible!!
Start
1 Coin = $....

Notes / Plans

52 Weeks
Savings
Challenges
HOUSE

Saving $1000 in 52 Weeks

Start date : __/__/____ Finish date : __/__/____

Great!!

$25 $20 $30 $15

$30 $10 $10 $10 $20 $20

$30 $15 $40 $35 $20 $10

$10 $20 $10 $15 $15 $10 $40 $10

$10 $20 $40 $25 $20 $25 $20 $15

$25 $10 $10 $25 $10 $10 $10 $35

$10 $25 $10 $10 $10 $35

$30 $30 $10 $10 $25 $15

Let's Start Here

1 Shape = 1 Week

Saving $1000 in 52 Weeks

Start date : __/__/____   Finish date : __/__/____

Excellent Job!!

| $20 | $30 | $10 | $10 | $15 | $40 | $35 | $20 |

| $10 | $10 | $20 | $10 | $15 | $10 | $10 | $15 |

| $20 | $10 | $20 | $30 | $20 | $30 | $15 | $10 |

| $40 | $10 | $10 | $20 | $40 | $25 |

| $20 | $35 | $25 | $15 | $25 | $25 |

| $10 | $35 | $10 | $25 | $10 | $10 |

| $10 | $25 | $10 | $30 | $10 | $30 |

| $10 | $25 | $10 | $15 |

Start Here

1 Shape = 1 Week

Saving $2000 in 52 Weeks

Start date : __/__/____   Finish date : __/__/____

Excellent Work!!

$55	$35		
$55	$50		
$57	$37	$55	$56
$45	$35	$50	$49
$48	$36	$45	$31
$47	$25	$44	$50
$44	$25	$48	$18
$40	$25	$40	$58
$35	$25	$35	$32
$25	$39	$36	$20
$35	$25	$33	$30
$22	$20	$30	$20
$28	$20	$55	$56
$22	$34	$60	$60

Start

1 Shape = 1 Week

Saving $2000 in 52 Weeks

Start date : __/__/____   Finish date : __/__/____

1 Plant = 1 Week

Saving $3000 in 52 Weeks

Start date : __/__/____ Finish date : __/__/____

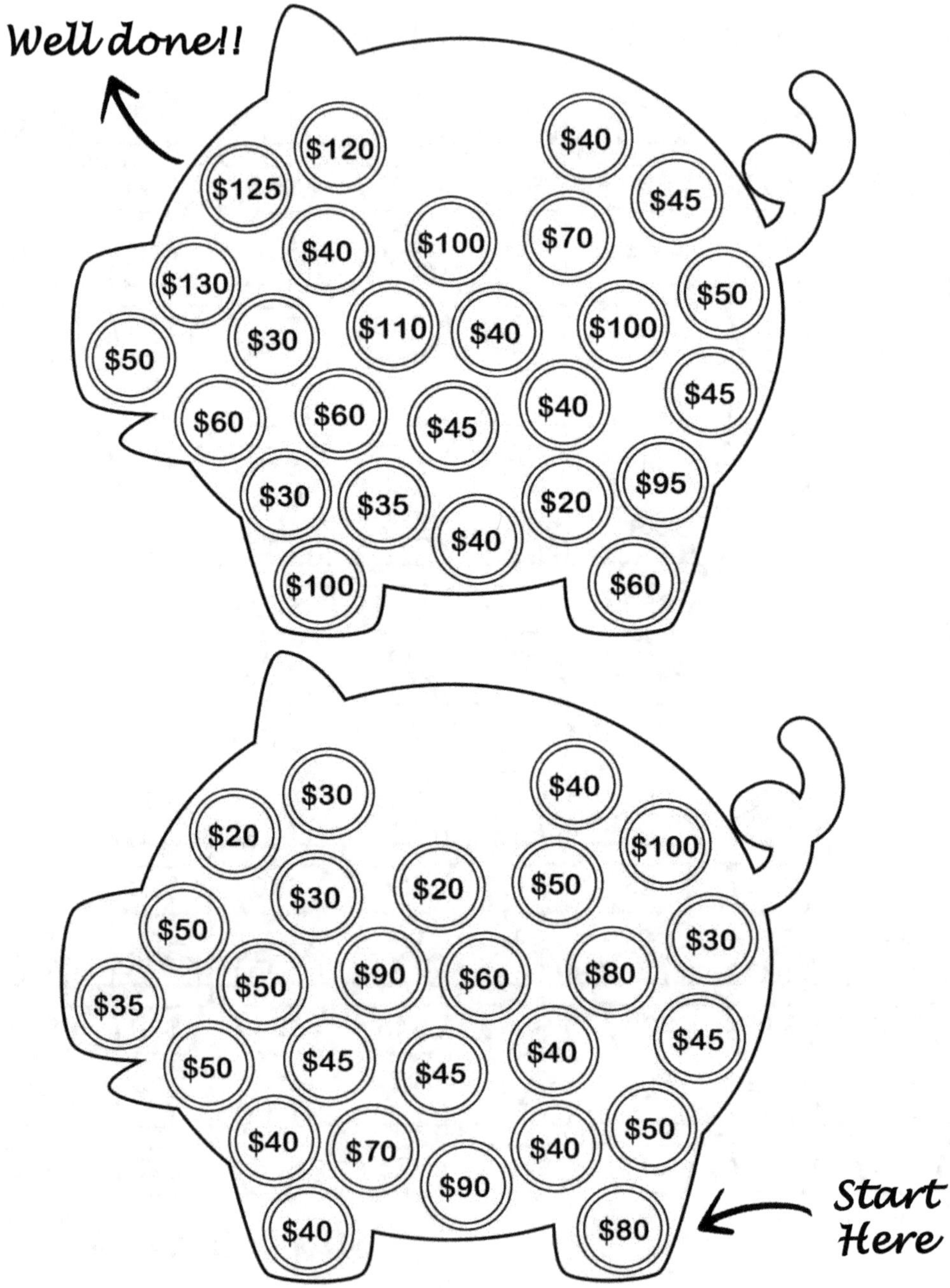

1 Coin = 1 Week

Saving $3000 in 52 Weeks

Start date : __/__/____ Finish date : __/__/____

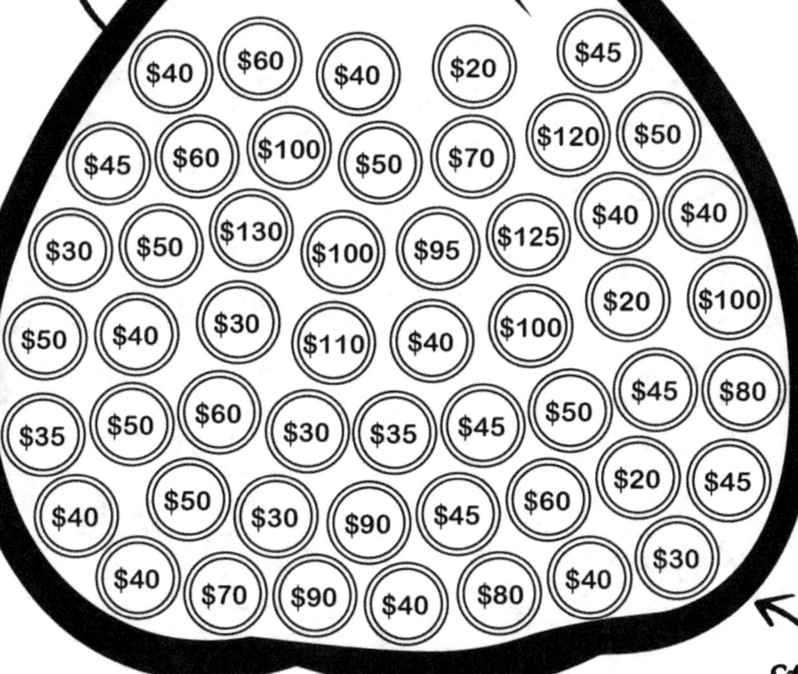

1 Coin = 1 Week

Saving $4000 in 52 Weeks

Start date : __/__/____ Finish date : __/__/____

Great!! ←

$120	$35	$55	$50	$60	$100
$55	$115	$90	$80	$50	$75
$80	$100	$60	$70	$120	$80	$130
$50	$90	$50	$75	$115	$70	$85
$40	$120	$65	$75	$95	$80	$75
$100	$95	$60	$35	$60	$110	$30
$100	$20	$30	$60	$125	$50
$55	$110	$115	$115	$60	$60

Start ↑

1 Plant = 1 Week

Saving $4000 in 52 Weeks

Start date : __/__/____   Finish date : __/__/____

Super Work!! ←

		$120		
	$35	$55	$50	
$60	$100	$55	$115	$90
$80	$50	$75	$80	$100
$60	$70	$120	$80	$130
$50	$90	$50	$75	$115
$70	$85	$40	$120	$65
$75	$95	$80	$75	$100
$95	$60	$35	$60	$110
$30	$100	$20	$30	$60
$125	$50	$55	$110	$115
	$115	$60	$60	

Start Here ↖

1 Shape = 1 Week

Saving $5000 in 52 Weeks
Start date : __/__/____   Finish date : __/__/____
Good Job!!
$120 $135 $155 $50
$60 $100 $155 $115 $90 $80
$150 $75 $80 $100 $60 $70 $120 $80
$130 $150 $90 $50 $75 $115 $70 $85
$40 $120 $65 $75 $95 $80 $95 $100
$95 $60 $135 $100 $110 $30 $100 $120
$30 $60 $125 $50 $155 $110
$115 $115 $100 $160
Start
1 Apple = 1 Week

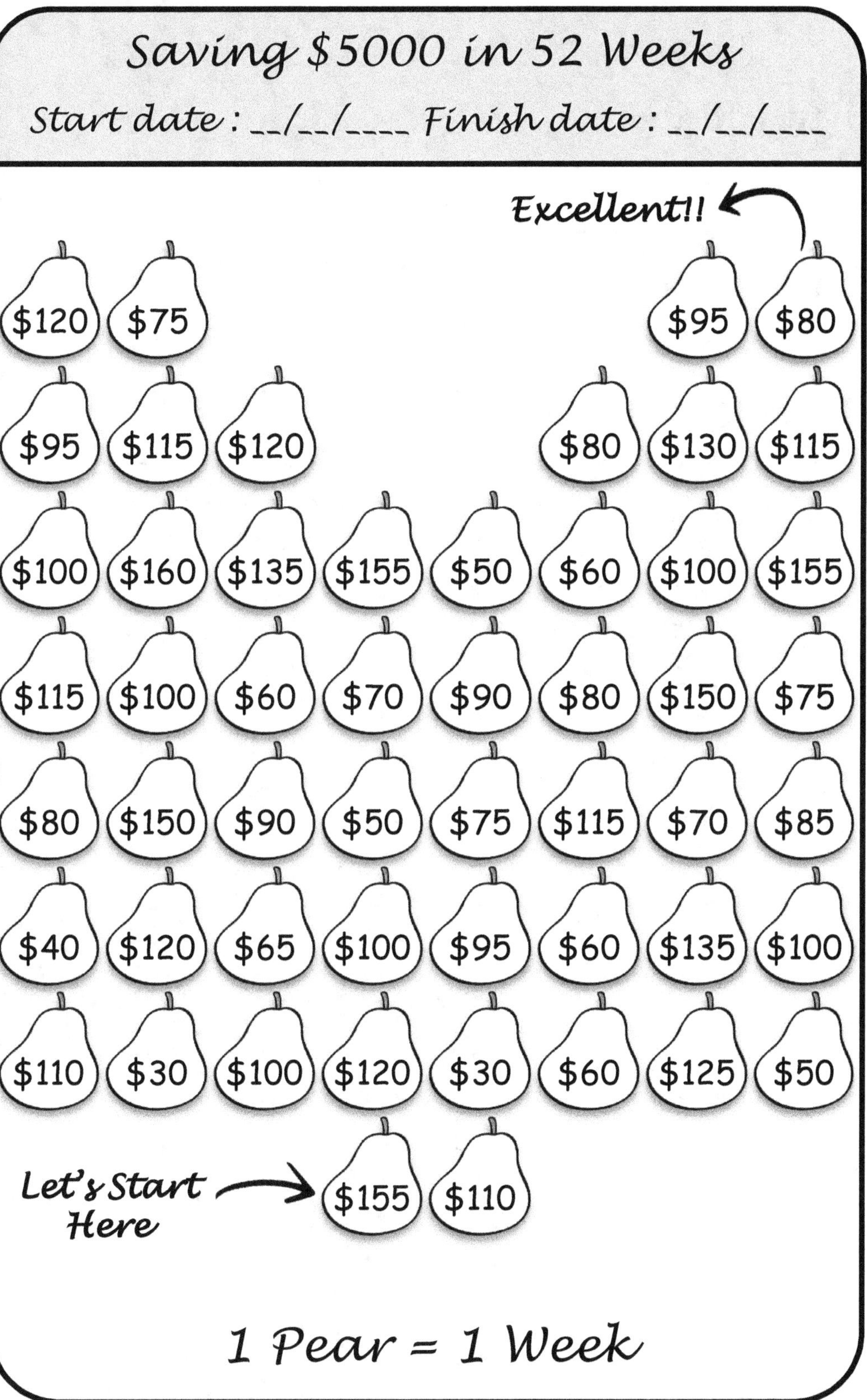

Saving $5000 in 52 Weeks
Start date : __/__/____ Finish date : __/__/____
Excellent!!
$120 $75
$95 $80
$95 $115 $120
$80 $130 $115
$100 $160 $135 $155 $50 $60 $100 $155
$115 $100 $60 $70 $90 $80 $150 $75
$80 $150 $90 $50 $75 $115 $70 $85
$40 $120 $65 $100 $95 $60 $135 $100
$110 $30 $100 $120 $30 $60 $125 $50
Let's Start Here
$155 $110
1 Pear = 1 Week

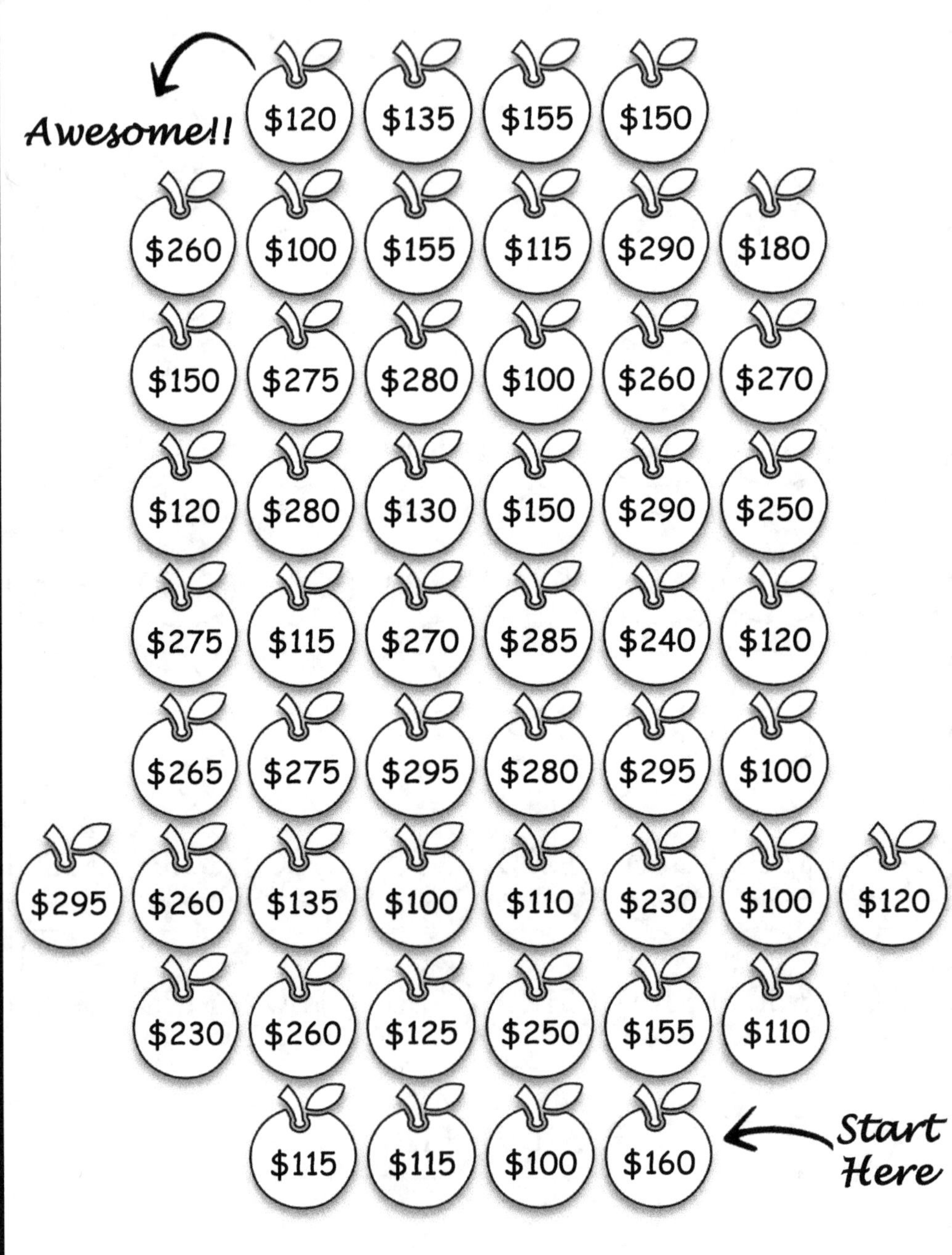

Saving $10.000 in 52 Weeks
Start date : __/__/____   Finish date : __/__/____
Awesome!!
$120
$135
$155
$150
$260
$100
$155
$115
$290
$180
$150
$275
$280
$100
$260
$270
$120
$280
$130
$150
$290
$250
$275
$115
$270
$285
$240
$120
$265
$275
$295
$280
$295
$100
$295
$260
$135
$100
$110
$230
$100
$120
$230
$260
$125
$250
$155
$110
$115
$115
$100
$160
Start Here
1 Orange = 1 Week

Saving $10.000 in 52 Weeks

Start date : __/__/____ Finish date : __/__/____

Incredible!!

$120 $150

$120 $280 $125 $260

$100 $155 $115 $290 $240 $120

$275 $265 $135 $100 $110 $230 $155 $180

$150 $275 $280 $100 $260 $270 $250 $130

$150 $115 $270 $285 $290 $250

$275 $295 $280 $295 $100 $295

$260 $135 $100 $120 $230 $260

$155 $115 $110 $115 $100 $160

Start

1 Lemon = 1 Week

Saving $15.000 in 52 Weeks
Start date : __/__/____ Finish date : __/__/____
Super!!
$320
$335
$355
$350
$260
$200
$255
$315
$290
$280
$250
$275
$280
$200
$260
$270
$340
$280
$330
$350
$290
$350
$275
$315
$270
$285
$240
$300
$265
$275
$295
$280
$295
$290
$295
$260
$335
$200
$320
$330
$310
$320
$330
$260
$325
$250
$255
$200
$315
$225
$290
$360
Start
Here
1 Watermelon = 1 Week

Saving $15.000 in 52 Weeks

Start date : __/__/____   Finish date : __/__/____

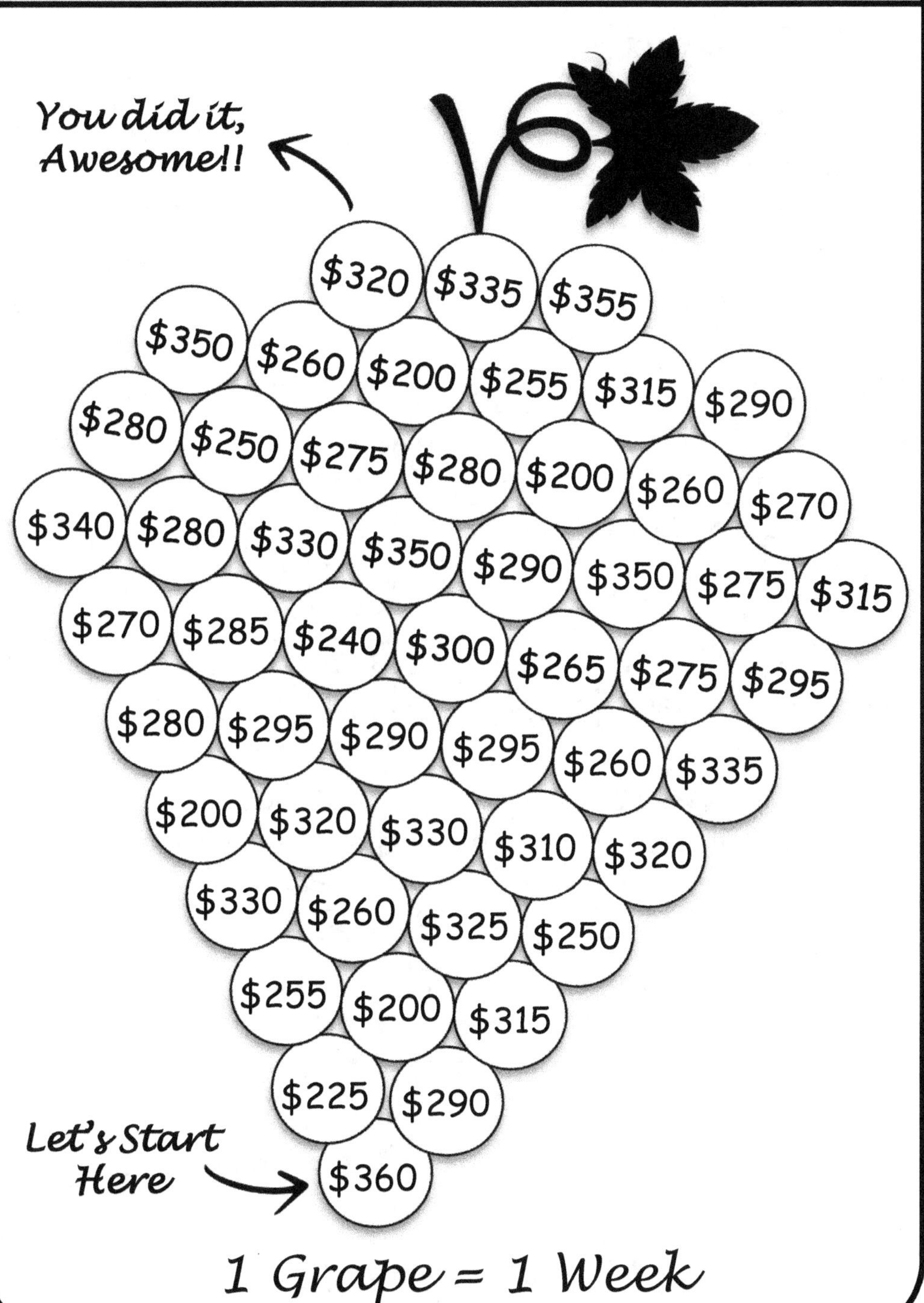

1 Grape = 1 Week

Saving $20.000 in 52 Weeks

Start date : __/__/____   Finish date : __/__/____

$420 $435

$355 $450

$260 $400 $355

$415 $390 $380

$450 $375 $280 $300 $360 $370 $340 $380 $330

$450 $290 $350 $375 $415 $370 $385 $440 $300

$465 $375 $395 $380 $395 $390 $295 $360 $435

$300 $420 $430 $410 $420 $430 $460

$425 $450 $455 $400 $415

$425 $290 $360

1 Jar = 1 Week

Saving $20.000 in 52 Weeks

Start date : __/__/____   Finish date : __/__/____

1 Cup = 1 Week

Set your own challenge
Saving $..... In 52 Weeks
Start date : __/__/____ Finish date : __/__/____
Great!
Let's Start Here
1 Plant = $....

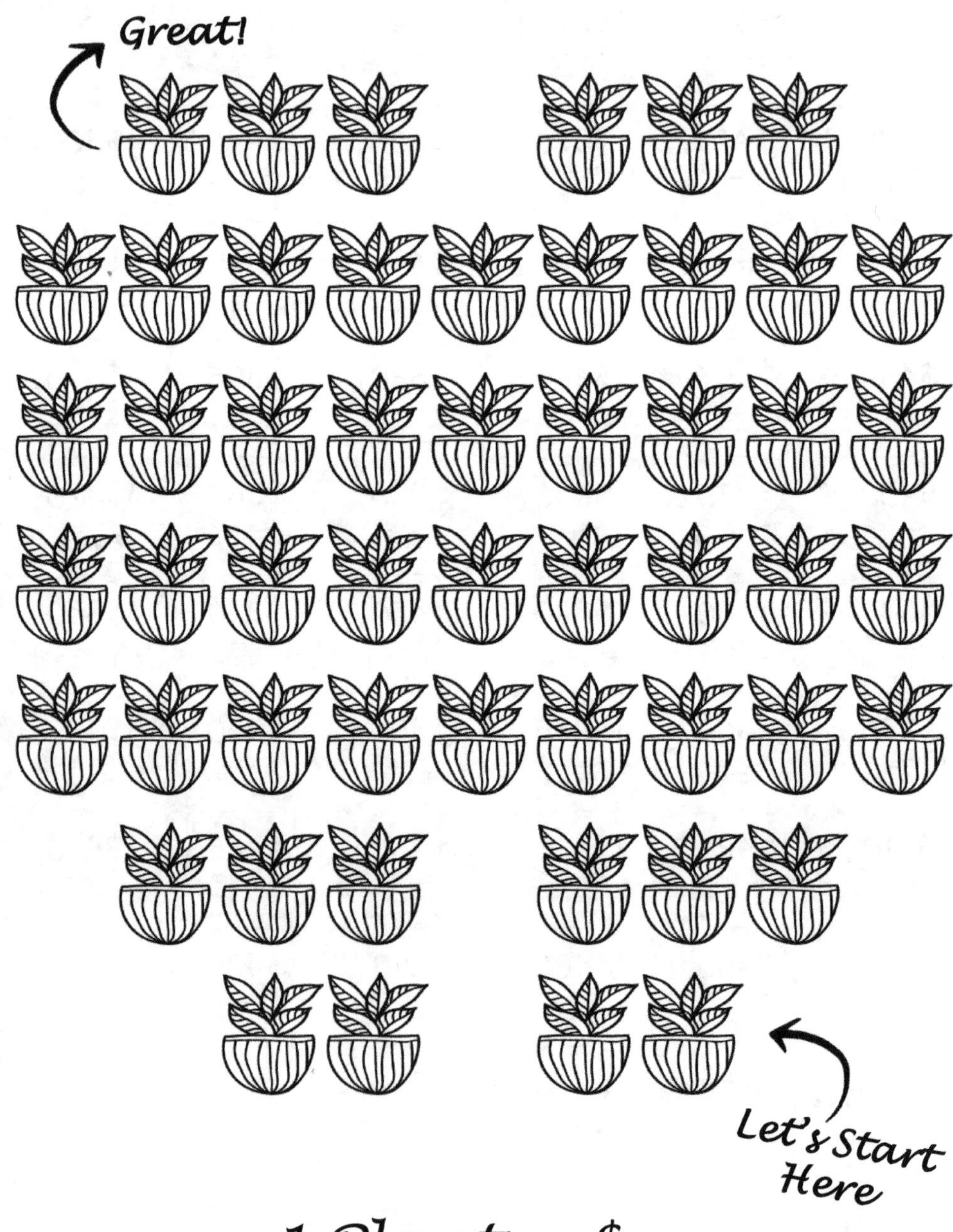

Set your own challenge
Saving $..... In 52 Weeks
Start date : __/__/____ Finish date : __/__/____
Great Job!!
Let's Start Here
1 Leaf = $....

Set your own challenge
Saving $..... In 52 Weeks

Start date : __/__/____   Finish date : __/__/____

1 Bottle = $....

Set your own challenge
Saving $..... In 52 Weeks
Start date : __/__/____   Finish date : __/__/____

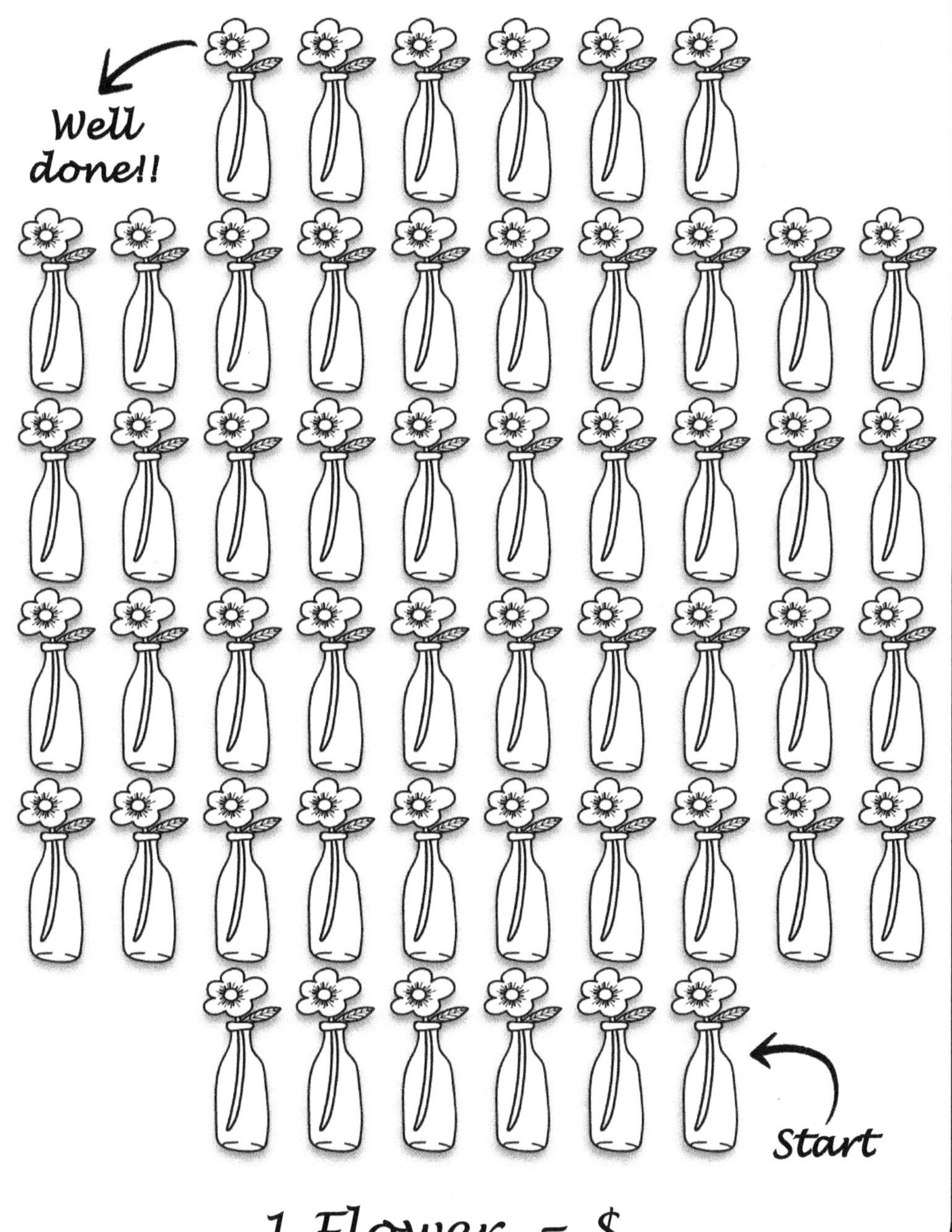

Extra Notes

Extra Notes

Extra Notes

Extra Notes

Extra Notes

Extra Notes

Extra Notes

Extra Notes

Extra Notes

Extra Notes

Extra Notes

Extra Notes

Extra Notes

Extra Notes

Extra Notes